# DAILY
# PRACTICES
*of*
# INCLUSIVE
# LEADERS

# DAILY PRACTICES

*of*

# INCLUSIVE LEADERS

A Guide to Building a

Culture of Belonging

**EDDIE PATE** *and*
**JONATHAN STUTZ**

Berrett–Koehler Publishers, Inc

Berrett-Koehler Publishers, Inc.
1333 Broadway, Suite 1000
Oakland, CA 94612-1921
Tel: (510) 817-2277
Fax: (510) 817-2278
www.bkconnection.com

ORDERING INFORMATION

**Quantity sales.** Special discounts are available on quantity purchases by corporations, associations, and others. For details, contact the "Special Sales Department" at the Berrett-Koehler address above.

**Individual sales.** Berrett-Koehler publications are available through most bookstores. They can also be ordered directly from Berrett-Koehler: Tel: (800) 929-2929; Fax: (802) 864-7626; www.bkconnection.com.

**Orders for college textbook / course adoption use.** Please contact Berrett-Koehler: Tel: (800) 929-2929; Fax: (802) 864-7626.

Distributed to the U.S. trade and internationally by Penguin Random House Publisher Services.

Berrett-Koehler and the BK logo are registered trademarks of Berrett-Koehler Publishers, Inc.

Printed in Canada

Berrett-Koehler books are printed on long-lasting acid-free paper. When it is available, we choose paper that has been manufactured by environmentally responsible processes. These may include using trees grown in sustainable forests, incorporating recycled paper, minimizing chlorine in bleaching, or recycling the energy produced at the paper mill.

Library of Congress Cataloging-in-Publication Data

Names: Pate, Eddie, author. | Stutz, Jonathan, author.
Title: Daily practices of inclusive leaders : a guide to building a culture of belonging / Eddie Pate and Jonathan Stutz.
Description: First Edition. | Oakland, CA : Berrett-Koehler Publishers, [2024] | Includes bibliographical references and index.
Identifiers: LCCN 2023049969 (print) | LCCN 2023049970 (ebook) | ISBN 9781523006410 (paperback) | ISBN 9781523006427 (pdf) | ISBN 9781523006434 (epub)
Subjects: LCSH: Diversity in the workplace—Management. | Personnel management. | Leadership.
Classification: LCC HF5549.5.M5 P38 2024 (print) | LCC HF5549.5.M5 (ebook) | DDC 658.30089—dc23/eng/20231027
LC record available at https://lccn.loc.gov/2023049969
LC ebook record available at https://lccn.loc.gov/2023049970

First Edition

31 30 29 28 27 26 25 24          10 9 8 7 6 5 4 3 2 1

Words and music to "Black & Blue" copyright © 2020 by Danny Schmidt. Reprinted by permission of the artist.

Book producer: Susan Geraghty
Text designer/typesetter: THE COSMIC LION
Cover designer: Daniel Tesser
Illustrations: Jaclyn Stutz-Burrick
Author Photograph: Rishi Lakshminarayanan

I dedicate this book, above all, to my loving and supportive family: Val, Karley, and Arthur. This doesn't happen without your inspiration, unwavering support, and caring. Much Love! To my mom, who I miss so much; I wish she were here to be a part of this moment. To my dad, who has always been there for me.

—*Eddie Pate*

To Stacie, the love of my life: this book is dedicated to you, for your enduring support, advice, and thoughtful consideration. It is your wisdom, heart, and courage that carry me.

—*Jonathan Stutz*

# Black & Blue

He was black and they were blue
The colors of a bruise
The colors of another brother
Who's choking on the truth

And so tonight the street's on fire
Cause that's the candlelight required
That's the holy cost of tape and chalk
That's the crying of the choir

Tell me why, there's another
Tell me why, in all this time
We're still defined by color
Tell me why

Tell me when, can the humble hearts of men bend
Bend and bow, and vow to disavow
Well tell me how,
Then tell me when

He was black and they were white
A cost without a price
A senseless flood of black men's blood
Now it's time to shed some light

And so tonight the streets are red
Marking every crooked bend
One by one the march goes on
Delivering the dead

Tell me why, there's another
Tell me why, in all this time
We're still defined by color
Tell me why

Tell me when, can the humble hearts of men bend
Bend and bow, and vow to disavow
Well tell me how,
Then tell me when

Cause I don't believe that victims go to heaven when they die
They're stuck here as reflections in our eyes
And of all the false confessions swearing that we've tried
They're the voice of silence asking when, and the voice that answers why

He was black and they were blue
The colors of abuse
The colors of another mother
Who's choked up on the news

And so we fight for streets of gold
Like we were promised and were told
To crown thy good with brotherhood
From soul to shining soul. Tell me why.

# Contents

# DAILY
# PRACTICES
*of*
# INCLUSIVE
# LEADERS

# Introduction

If you're reading this book, you're likely aware of the proliferation of diversity and inclusion initiatives in recent years. Organizations are investing real money and energy into making their workplaces equitable and accessible to employees of all backgrounds and abilities. The business case for inclusion, diversity, and equity (ID&E) has been made at the highest levels of most companies. However, the lived experience of a diverse workforce often seems far from the glossy pages of training books and company reports. And the gap between what has been promised and what is being delivered is undermining much of the progress that has been made.

Our book aims to close this gap.

There has been a consistent drumbeat from leaders, and it's getting louder. ID&E practitioners want to deliver programs that matter. They want leaders to be authentically engaged—not just as allies cheering loudly from the stands but as accomplices with skin in the game. Leaders also want to be engaged in meaningful ways, but they don't want to add more to their already overloaded plates.

Everyone wants to know the practical, daily actions they can take to create an inclusive work environment: leaders, ID&E practitioners, and the mass of incredibly passionate people who are doing ID&E work in cultural coalitions, diversity leadership teams, employee resource groups (ERGs), and other mission-driven groups.

Everyone wants to see their efforts pay off! This is where we come in.

It's important to state up front that we are not disrespecting the ID&E work that so many people have been doing for years, putting everything they've got into making a difference. Far from it. We applaud the work and understand that this book can only exist because of the efforts that preceded it. We acknowledge the shoulders we are standing on and, indeed, the perspectives we are using to help frame the message of *Daily Practices of Inclusive Leaders*.

We've witnessed the establishment of the irrefutable business case for ID&E. We've watched concepts such as inclusion, equity, unconscious bias, Inclusive Leadership, microinequities, microaggressions, and intersectionality gain sustainable footholds in the public consciousness. We've observed structural, systemic, and full life-cycle ID&E approaches finally move into everyday dialogue. Despite the pullback of late, with ID&E being used as fuel for a fabricated culture war, there has been substantial growth in dedicated resources, in the diversity of candidate pools, in organizational buy-in, and in legitimate dialogue. Folks around the globe are coming around to the realization that ID&E is *not* simply a US fad. It is a philosophy, a strategic imperative, and a real need everywhere.

But what we aren't seeing is the amount of impact we want. And certainly not at the pace of change we need.

Despite all the books and programs out there, the turnover of Black and Brown workers, the underemployment of people with disabilities, and the overall experience of other historically oppressed and marginalized people remain serious problems. Those are just a few examples.

We have heard the cry. Leaders need real, daily engagement practices that build a culture of belonging for every person.

Over the course of our careers, we have demonstrated that doing ID&E can be inspirational and practical. It can touch a global audience of everyday ID&E practitioners *and* engineers who want to develop their "soft" skills *and* community activists who want to have an impact. Our experience has shown us that the synthesis of a heart-centered, developed wisdom, courageous leadership style and the approach of using small but meaningful actions is the next definitive step for Inclusive Leadership to take hold.

Ultimately, inclusion doesn't come from the HR department, that training course you took, or the chief diversity officer. If you're a leader, it starts with you—what you do every day and how you create the expectation for others to play a part. But we believe you don't need to (and shouldn't) do this work alone. Therefore, we also provide the guidance to influence your peers, inspire those who report to you, and enable the people who want to partner with you in this work. The beauty of our approach is that it doesn't just work for HR professionals or influential leaders in the C-suite. It works for anyone with an empathetic resolve to do better and a willingness to personally own their part.

In *Daily Practices of Inclusive Leaders* you'll find a globally relevant tool kit of actions and behaviors that actually build a culture of belonging. You'll find proven daily practices for lifting up and increasing the visibility of the historically overlooked, such as running inclusive meetings; developing effective mentoring, recruiting, and engagement programs; and doing myriad other activities that structure the rhythm of your business.

Leading inclusively requires heart, courage, and a strong sense that everyone should have equitable access and the opportunity to thrive in their professional and personal lives. Here, we leverage Debra Meyerson's work on how leaders inspire change at work from her influential book, *Tempered Radicals: How Everyday Leaders Inspire Change at Work.*[1] Meyerson uses two analogies that we will reference throughout our book. She equates small, impactful actions to "dropping pebbles" that cause ripples, which cause more pebbles to be dropped and result in more ripples. The aggregation of these pebbles or small, impactful actions leads to systemic and cultural change. Meyerson also equates "rocking the boat" with the courage and heart needed to do what is right and not what is expected. Being a tempered radical means rocking the boat, but not so hard that you knock yourself and others out of the boat. You need to be in the boat to effect change. Like Meyerson, we want leaders to understand that they don't have to create an enormous change all at once. Instead, we ask leaders to drop a pebble of change, one that causes a ripple, which in turn motivates someone else to drop a pebble that also causes a ripple, which in turn motivates someone else to drop a pebble, and so on. It is the aggregation of all those pebbles that leads to waves of systemic change.

This is a big shift in how ID&E is practiced today—and a long overdue one. Breaking down the work into daily practices, what we call pebbles of inclusion, makes ID&E much more doable and sustainable for incredibly busy people. And it gets people excited! We've seen relief, excitement, and a new resolve in leaders when we've offered this framework during engagements and trainings. This approach to Inclusive Leadership has proven itself to be an effective means of empowering others to play a part.

## WHAT IS A DAILY PRACTICE OF INCLUSION?

*Practice* means to work repeatedly to become proficient to acquire or polish a skill. This is what inclusive leaders do well; they are lifelong learners who hone their skills every day to become increasingly effective at leading an increasingly globally diverse workforce. Daily practices of inclusion reflect the expectation that inclusion is a life-long practice—one that is part of the rhythm of the business and not a separate one-off effort.

A daily practice of inclusion is an inclusive action or behavior that is integrated into the way a leader operates on a daily basis. Each practice is informed by the leader's evolving awareness of the intersections of identity present in each human interaction and business decision. Each is a pebble that they drop into the sea of their organization's culture and that gradually causes ripple effects of change that build a culture of belonging. It is important to walk away from this section understanding just how significant this new approach is. So many leaders struggle with how to make ID&E effective, how to integrate this work into business strategies, and how and when to hold people in their organizations accountable. But there's never enough time, energy, or resources to do this work! The result? Defensiveness, sometimes testy attitudes and behaviors, and an obvious lack of support. Nobody needs more work that they don't have the time to do.

What makes this daily practice approach so effective is that leaders do not have to do it all. They simply need to practice—daily. All they need to do is drop pebbles that cause ripples and hold others accountable to do the same.

Imagine if twenty-five people in your organization dropped pebbles of inclusion, each of which caused a ripple. And those ripples encouraged fifty more people to drop pebbles, and so on. Before long you have a critical mass of pebbles (i.e., inclusive wins) that leads to systemic and organizational change. Quite literally, cultural change happens as the result of an aggregation of small wins.

It has been so gratifying to see lights go on when we explain this to leaders, leaders who've wanted to get engaged and do meaningful ID&E work but just could not figure out how it was possible.

## WHAT IS A CULTURE OF BELONGING?

We all can talk about feeling connected; we all can talk about feeling part of a greater purpose; we all can talk about feeling valued, supported, and heard. These are all important elements of belonging, but they're not the whole picture. The reality is that each person working for you has a different, very personal definition of what belonging means.

Building a culture of belonging begins with the day-to-day interactions between you and your team members. It includes taking the time to get to know each person at a deeper level—who they are, where they come from, what their experiences and backgrounds have taught them, and what makes them special and unique, besides what is on their resume. A culture of belonging develops over time from both formal and informal conversations, shared laughter and shared joy, collective accomplishments, struggles, failures, risks taken together, and highs and lows, both inside and outside of work. This trust built over time is what enables people to feel *I belong here.*

The daily practices of inclusion in this book are a guide to building a culture of belonging, something that is centrally important for people who have historically been left out, excluded, and made to feel as though they don't fit in at work. But the "breaking news" here is that these same daily practices help everyone feel more comfortable and part of the team.

Many innovations in disability technology have ultimately provided broad benefits for society. Think of audiobooks. The technology was developed in the 1930s for people with impaired vision as an alternative to Braille. The same goes for the curb cuts in sidewalks, which were originally developed for people who use wheelchairs, but have proven invaluable for people using bikes, strollers, scooters, skates, and walkers. Even the forerunner of Apple's Siri used text-to-speech software that was initially developed by inventor Ray Kurzweil with the National Federation for the Blind.

While folks often think that ID&E focuses only on people who have historically been underestimated, marginalized, or oppressed by society, diversity includes everyone. We all bring elements of diversity to work every day. We are so much more than our visible dimensions of diversity, such as race or gender, and each of us deserves to feel that we belong.

## WHY DO WE CALL IT ID&E?

Think for a moment of your place of work as a home. Before you invite people into your home, you typically want to ensure that your home is a safe, warm, welcoming place where people can be comfortable, can relax, and can be themselves. When they share thoughts and opinions, you don't want them to worry about being ridiculed or ostracized, or not fitting in. We believe that your organization should be as welcoming and as safe a place to work as your home would be for employees to visit. For this reason, we prioritize the importance of inclusion. Putting the *I* before the *D* and *E* is a gentle and intentional reminder of the primary importance of inclusion. It's a small pebble we're dropping that contributes to the ripples of change in thinking and in the culture.

## WHY WE USE THE PHRASE "DOMINANT GROUP"

Throughout the book, we use some variation of the phrase *dominant group*. You'll find *culturally dominant* or *dominant, majority culture* or *dominant demographic*. We use these phrases because in different geographies around the world, the dominant group varies. In the US, the dominant group with significant unearned privilege comprises white men; in other places, the dominant group may be made up of members of a religious or cultural designation, or lighter-skinned members of a society where color exerts a significant impact on outcomes, or men in general. The use of "dominant group" is our acknowledgment that the readership for this book is global.

## WHY WE WROTE THIS BOOK

To build teams and organizations that are exceptional, people must develop the skills and discipline to practice inclusion daily. Creating a work environment where everyone feels connected and supported, cares for one another, and gives unselfishly of themselves to one another begins with the leader who practices Inclusive Leadership. Daily.

We both identify as family-focused, proud parents and as people active in our communities with a lifelong commitment to inclusion, diversity, equity, and social justice. We both have had amazing lived experiences and ones that have challenged us as human beings.

Jonathan was born in Toronto, Canada, yet grew up in Atlanta, Georgia, during the height of the US civil rights movement. In the Deep South, Jonathan was raised in the Jewish faith and his early education instilled the social action and social justice concept of Tikkun Olam deep in his being. Tikkun Olam refers to various forms of action intended to repair and improve the world.

Jonathan first became aware of his Jewish identity through his religious education—and the teasing and bullying he experienced in elementary school in 1960s Atlanta. Through those formative years, Jonathan endured antisemitic jokes and name-calling while observing the parents of his "friends" using racist and hateful language toward Black people. He heard adults call Martin Luther King Jr. a "troublemaker." On carpool drives to Pop Warner youth football practices, he recalls the father of a teammate referring to Black people as "coons" and using the "n-word." Yet at home, his family shared values dedicated to civil rights, actively working against discrimination. Jonathan's mother volunteered within the segregated Black schools teaching second-grade children to read and write. His older brother and mentor, Brian, worked on political campaigns supporting candidates whose values and actions were consistent with the Jewish value of Tikkun Olam.

When Jonathan was ten years old, he and his family moved to Mercer Island, Washington, in the Seattle area. He later went on to study political science and history at the University of Washington, worked on political campaigns himself, and aspired to live a life dedicated to addressing inequity and social injustice wherever he saw it.

> I found my life's work when I joined Microsoft's first
> diversity team in the mid-1990s. It ignited the pilot
> light that had been burning since my childhood expe-
> riences in Atlanta.

Since then, Jonathan has worked to learn about and understand the lived experiences of underestimated, marginalized, and oppressed people. He's traveled globally in this quest, doing business in nearly twenty-five different countries.

Eddie is a military brat born in Frankfurt, Germany, on a US Army base to a mixed-race couple. (Dad is Black, and Mom is white.) He grew up at a time when interracial marriage was still illegal in many of the states where he and his family lived, and was unacceptable almost everywhere. The first military base the family came to in the US was in Georgia, where Eddie's mom was told that for her and her mixed-race kids' safety she should not leave the army base with them. This was the zeitgeist that prevailed during much of Eddie's childhood and into his adult life.

While Eddie strongly identifies as Black, he has had a complex lived experience in which at times he wasn't Black enough or was clearly too Black. It's been a point of continuous reflection for him, and one that fueled his passion for ID&E. The disconnect between what should be and what was and is reality for so many Black and Brown people also weighs heavily on him. What these lived experiences did for Eddie was to plant the seeds in his mind that grew into an unquenchable thirst for social justice, inclusion, and empathy.

> I've always been someone who confidently moved toward things that were hard. I've also always wanted to find ways to help others with similar life experiences, to help others who are not a part of underestimated or oppressed populations understand and play their part in fixing what is wrong. I genuinely work to leave whatever we have now better than when I experienced it. These are all powerful drivers for me.

Our collective experiences growing up as the "other" definitely influenced what we did for work, how we think, and the positive impact we passionately want to make. Writing this book just may have been destiny. We talked multiple times over our years together working at Amazon about writing a book on Inclusive Leadership. The topic came up on a business trip to India we took together, during one-to-one meetings in each of our offices at Amazon, and during the many times we were reflecting on societal woes and the challenges in doing ID&E work. Those conversations continued after we both "soft-retired" from full-time work and started our respective ID&E consulting companies. Thanks to an introduction from Jonathan's close friend Bill Price, an opportunity with Berrett-Koehler Publishers landed in front of us;

we jumped on it. We have a combined fifty-plus years of experience driving ID&E efforts, leading geopolitical teams and change management, influencing without authority (as so many ID&E leaders must do), and engaging in meaningful and often tense discussions with everyone from entry-level employees to CEOs.

We've done this work at some incredible companies: Microsoft, Starbucks, Zulily, Avanade, and Amazon—all of which pushed us to think globally and act locally. We had to figure out how to scale efforts across hundreds of thousands of employees and hundreds of teams. At every point, we built teams from scratch. We've both leveraged our academic backgrounds in our work. Jonathan has an extensive background studying leadership, cross-cultural communication, and change management, earning a bachelor of arts in political science from the University of Washington and a master of arts in organizational leadership from City University of Seattle. Eddie focused on macro- and microlevel race and ethnicity dynamics, earning a master of arts in sociology from Humboldt State University and a PhD from the University of Washington in sociology, comparative race and ethnic relations, and social psychology.

This book is a continuation of both of our journeys, our passion for ID&E, and our sincere desire, as cliché as this sounds, to have a meaningful and sustained impact. As this book is a collaborative effort, we've chosen to write it using the collective voice of "we" throughout, unless otherwise noted.

We want to lead from the front and evolve the dialogue surrounding Inclusive Leadership. We hope our contribution to this crucial topic will also give leadership theorists and practitioners a new framework to consider and integrate into their work. We believe that our approach nests nicely into leadership style frameworks that espouse servant leadership, empathetic leadership, participative leadership, and transformational leadership styles. In essence, we believe that Inclusive Leadership is leadership.

Our goal is for the leaders and decision-makers who follow this framework to enjoy higher levels of retention, greater employee engagement, a stronger sense of belonging among *all* employees, and, as the business case for diversity argues quite successfully, more creativity and innovation.

## WHAT'S IN THIS BOOK

This book is written for an audience of ID&E enthusiasts. Whether it's part of your job responsibilities or not, you understand the case for ID&E and are passionate about building a culture of belonging at your organization. You may or may not have the authority within your organization to create structural change, but you're excited to begin dropping the daily pebbles of inclusion that lead to it.

We assume that you have a functional, working knowledge of inclusion, diversity, equity, intersectionality, and intentionality. We will therefore define key concepts as needed, but there won't be a focused chapter on the basics. Our goal is to be laser focused on the day-to-day practical, globally contextual actions, activities, and programs you need to lead inclusively with impact—actions that have a ripple effect and that contribute to waves of change.

We assume you're here because you already know the what and the why, and now you're ready to learn the how. We're here to show it to you.

In part 1, we share the foundations of Inclusive Leadership. It starts with a vision of an inclusive team working in a culture of belonging. Then, you need the wisdom—the *how* of leading a diverse workforce. Here we dive deep into our Inclusive Leadership model, including our seven insights for lifelong learning. Next, we focus on the daily practice of standing up for inclusion and inspiring others to do the same. Courage is central to building a culture of belonging. We complete the foundational elements by sharing the importance of heart to the Inclusive Leadership journey. Demonstrating heart to your people is how you build trust; it creates the psychological safety that makes people feel okay to show up as they are. Part 1 culminates with the last of the foundational elements, structure and accountability, which accelerates the ability of an organization to build a culture of belonging. Scattered throughout, you will find profiles of real-life leaders we have worked with who embody the wisdom, heart, courage, and daily practice of Inclusive Leadership.

In part 2, we explore the daily practices that can interrupt the natural human tendencies that prevent leaders from building a culture of belonging. We grow your awareness and understanding of these human behaviors that impact how people treat others different from them at each stage of the employee life cycle—recruiting, hiring, developing, engaging, and promoting. We share the daily practices of inclusion that you and your employees can use to slow down and think critically about why you're making the decisions you're making. Last, we discuss the inevitable hurdles you will face on your Inclusive Leadership journey and offer practical tools and tips for navigating them.

At the end of the book, we provide our guiding principles to help you make ripples as an inclusive leader. We also address how to sustain ID&E efforts in the face of the attacks around the globe on programs and people working for progress on inclusion, equity, and justice.

As we write this book in the summer and fall of 2023, it feels as though we're experiencing a legitimization of overt white supremacy[2]— at least here in the US. In the US, states such as Florida and Texas are banning books[3] that promote diversity and threatening to pull educational funding from universities seeking to diversify their student bodies. Systemic racism continues to fuel the murdering of Black and Brown people in the US, and the efforts to completely disenfranchise these groups through voter suppression[4] and gerrymandering.[5] There has also been a surge in Asian hate crimes across the US since the COVID-19 pandemic in response to rhetoric about the origins of this deadly virus.[6] According to the Pew Research Center, about one-third of Asian adults (32 percent) say they personally know an Asian person in the US who has been threatened or attacked because of their race or ethnicity since the pandemic began.[7]

A shocking increase in antisemitism was noted in 2022 with 3,697 incidents in the US alone that year, a 36 percent increase from the previous year and the highest ever recorded since the Anti-Defamation League (ADL) began tracking in 1979.[8] In 2023, the war between Hamas and Israel caused historic increases in harassment, vandalism, and assault affecting Jewish, Muslim, and Palestinian Arab communities. Preliminary data from the ADL Center on Extremism indicate that reported incidents of anti-Jewish harassment, vandalism and assault increased by 388 percent over the same period in the prior year.[9] The American-Arab Anti-Discrimination Committee reported increases in violence, threats, and harassment of Muslims and Arabs not seen since 2016 amid Trump's rise, which surpassed the previous peak from 9/11.[10] With organizations being a microcosm of our society at large, we are 100 percent certain that the fallout from all of this will make what leaders do to create systemic and cultural change harder yet even more critical. And we don't even know yet what the full impact of the US Supreme Court's 2023 decisions on Affirmative Action and Free Speech will be.

The very need for ID&E work in communities, companies, and organizations is being challenged—which makes what leaders do even more imperative. We all need to lead inclusively and build a culture of belonging so that everyone, no matter the diversity they bring—and because of the diversity they bring—can do their best work, achieve their maximum potential, and enable organizations to perform at the highest levels. This is how everybody wins.

Let's go!

# Part 1

## THE FOUNDATIONS

## OF INCLUSIVE

## LEADERSHIP

I nclusive leaders understand that how they show up matters. How they represent who they are matters. How they listen matters. How their understanding of their experiences and the experiences of others matters. How they take ownership for their actions—every day—matters.

Over the course of the next five chapters, we push you to wrestle with the profound implications of Martin Luther King Jr.'s powerful words, "Our lives begin to end the day we become silent about things that matter."[1]

We lay the framework for what it takes for inclusive leaders to lead sustainable culture change. We share our Insights of Inclusive Leadership (2IL) model, which in combination with heart, courage, structure, and accountability is the foundation for how leaders can build a culture of belonging, a place where every individual supports and values every other individual. We dispel the myth that ID&E work needs to be overwhelming and all-consuming. Last, we illustrate the power of collective action within organizations, one pebble and one ripple at a time.

# Chapter 1

# WHY LEADERS ARE KEY TO THE DAILY PRACTICE OF INCLUSION

## Ed Salcedo on Inclusive Leadership

Edward Salcedo is the founder and president of GCAP Services Inc., a Hispanic-owned small-business professional consulting firm headquartered in Costa Mesa, California. These are the five core principles that inform Ed's Inclusive Leadership style.

### 1. Listen. Be humble. Gain input from everyone.

*Keep an open mind; listen without judgment. To listen is so powerful. Be silent. Then when you speak, tell them what you are hearing. People want to be respected. Their voices are just as important as anyone else's*

A few years back, Ed's company, GCAP Services, changed its employee performance evaluations to include an employee self-assessment and manager assessment. The leadership wanted to learn from their people what they enjoyed doing, where they wanted to grow, and how they wanted their managers to support them. They created a safe space for people to voice their ideas, opinions, and perspectives. Ed's thinking was that a small company like GCAP may not be able to fulfill every employee need, but it can help people gain experience in the areas they are interested in and help them on the path to where they want to go. The results have been extremely positive. Employees were spot-on in their self-assessments, making the whole feedback process much smoother. They knew where they needed to improve and what they needed to grow. "It was so much better for them to tell us. We're listening to them explain how they can be better, instead of us just telling them what we want."

## 2. Share information with employees.

> It's important for people to understand what I do as president of GCAP. I want to give people the knowledge to learn, to understand, to think about, and to plan what we're doing as a company.

Ed believes GCAP has benefited from its culture of cascading information to everyone, which then enables information to cascade up to leadership. That way, learning happens at all levels of the organization.

## 3. Share information with business partners.

> If you are always calling and asking your business partners for something, after a while, they're not going to take your calls. But if you're calling to give them something that they are interested in, it creates an environment where people want to hear from you. You establish a great relationship, and they are happy to share if you need any help.

When Ed and his staff obtain information from a social or business event, they go out of their way to share it. They'll intentionally share business leads and opportunities with people in GCAP's network: business partners, consultants, and even competitors. And they never have any expectation of getting something back in return. Ed believes it's one reason GCAP gets so many new opportunities. A partner will send information over saying, "I think this is closer to what you do than us" because they trust that GCAP will do the same for them.

## 4. Give people a chance.

*Give them the tools, be there for them, and get out of the way. I'm not quick to correct unless someone's factually wrong. I'm a macromanager not a micromanager.*

Early in Ed's career, Tony DeLuca, the former CEO of the $1.5 billion IT Group Inc., served as his manager and mentor. Tony put his trust in Ed, giving him a chance to lead a new subsidiary, even though Ed didn't have much experience in those days. Tony treated people with respect and gave them opportunities to prove themselves. And now Ed is paying it forward.

For Ed, giving people a chance extends to appreciating their different ways of doing things. He gives them the opportunity to bring their own style to their work. He loves to train and teach his staff, but once they're up and running, he pulls back, letting them do their good work, unencumbered by management oversight.

## 5. Participate in social justice initiatives.

*If you can provide a little nugget, a little bit of knowledge about what's going on in other, less privileged communities, you can have a huge impact on people.*

The social injustices in the US that were brought to the forefront over the last several years changed Ed's leadership. They made him aware of what he needed to do externally in his community and internally at GCAP to be a part of the solution. Ed started participating in professional groups such as the Stanford Latino Entrepreneurship Initiative, providing Latine entrepreneurs with help in scaling their business. He joined the Orange County (CA) Hispanic Chamber of Commerce supporting youth educational programs. GCAP also now sponsors scholarships earmarked to help Latine students get through school. And inside GCAP, they've implemented daily practices of inclusion dedicated to building a strong culture of belonging. A daily practice that Ed adopted to ensure that he hears everyone's perspective is to ask folks who haven't spoken up in a meeting, "Brittany, do you have anything to add? Sarah? Jaime?" This practice supports his belief in respecting everyone's opinion and collecting information from everyone.

It's been said that a society is measured by how it treats its most vulnerable members. We can say the same about companies and all organizations.

How are you treating your most vulnerable employees? Ask yourself: How livable is our work environment? How healthy is the culture? How are our most vulnerable employees doing? Are they thriving or struggling? Are they getting promoted? Are they being seen, heard, valued, and understood? Do I know?

Employees who feel isolated and alone find it incredibly challenging to perform at the same level as those employees who feel a connection. It's especially important for leaders to understand that employees who don't feel supported, are not included in lunch or after-work social activities, are overlooked for key developmental programs, or are the last to find out about decisions impacting them directly will end up feeling more isolated and alone. Ultimately, there's a greater likelihood that their morale will drop, they'll become dejected and disengaged, and they'll be less creative. These are the employees who are most likely to leave—either by their choice or yours. Our daily practices of inclusion will help you bring everyone into the fold and increase retention of the talented people you worked so hard to recruit.

It took years for it to crystallize for us that leaders were a critical piece of the ID&E puzzle. Perhaps had we come to this conclusion sooner, we would have had even more impact along the way. But no, this understanding was built slowly over the initial years of our work in the ID&E space: leaders need to lead inclusively for all the pieces to fit together.

The clues were there, and the people who modeled Inclusive Leadership were there for us to interact with and learn from. Take Charles Stevens, former VP of the Enterprise Partner Group at Microsoft. Way back in 2000, twenty-plus years ago, he set in motion huge change by making the group's new diversity manager a direct report. This was a first at Microsoft. It was a major signal that ID&E was more than just an HR initiative. This significant move and the subsequent ripples led to, among other things, an intense discussion of the importance of diversity resources and where they should sit. The new role planted the seed in the minds of other senior leaders that diversity was something important to integrate into the work they do. It also spurred the creation of the first Microsoft Women's Conference, which is still held annually to this day.

Stevens understood that diversity, especially within a global sales organization, should be a critical piece of any business strategy. He took action as a response to that understanding, which led to systemic change and became for us the first glimmers of what leading inclusively looked like.

(As a quick side note, we purposely wrote "diversity" here and not "inclusion, diversity, and equity" because in and around 2000, that is how we referred to what we did. We were diversity professionals.)

## LEADING WITH YOUR EARS

Leaders are key to achieving a sense of belonging, yet how? It's certainly not one or two big programs that build a culture of belonging. Leaders who make a deliberate effort every day to listen deeply to their people with a genuine intent to understand have an edge. We call this *leading with your ears*. These leaders ask open-ended questions. They take the time to hear people's stories and about their life experiences, to learn their goals and aspirations. They create the space for employees to feel safe showing up as they really are.

A leader should get to know their people and connect with each person on both a professional and personal level. This is one of the core elements of building a strong culture of belonging. If you've ever been fortunate to work on one of those special teams where everyone knows their role, everyone feels connected to each other, and tapping into each person's knowledge, skills, and abilities is a seamless process, you know what we mean. Each person feels confident they are seen, heard, valued, and understood. They truly feel they belong on that team. It's an "I've got your back and you've got mine" culture.

Over time, leaders can develop that level of trust, connection, and understanding. It starts with knowing your people's needs and then having the insight to help them achieve their goals. It involves cultivating a collective vision for the future and then applying that vision to every person on the team. It requires coaching and guiding through day-to-day interactions that take your people from where they are to where they want to be. By getting to know everyone personally and becoming a partner in their career journey, you begin to build a culture of belonging. And as a result, each person will work harder, be more loyal and more committed, and perform at a higher level.

One of the reasons it's so critical to spend time getting to know your people at a deeper level is that all of us so often default to some story we create in our minds about people's background, culture, ethnicity, gender, ability, or skills. Based on the very nature of how our minds work and the experiences we've had, the books we've read or movies we've seen, the news, the media in general, our parents, our families, our teachers, and all the positive and negative experiences we've had up until now, we zone in on this single one-dimensional story of a person.

Can you see the discrepancies between being an inclusive leader and using single stories to make critical people decisions?

At the beginning of each Inclusive Leadership course we teach, we have participants watch the influential TED Talk of author Chimamanda Ngozi Adichie titled "The Danger of a Single Story."[1] You can use the next QR code to access the video. From the many times we've watched this video, we've learned along with our participants just how vulnerable we all are to the single story about a person or a particular group of people or even a company, especially when they are different from us.

All leaders, us included, have single stories that may influence how we perceive someone's ability and whom we hire, promote, and fire. It's important to be aware of this possibility. In Adichie's TED Talk, she emphasizes how power plays a factor. Those in positions of power and privilege have a greater ability to control the narrative, whether that be via the media or through access to other people in positions of power, such as politicians or senior leadership in the organization. But no matter what position we hold, we all can be trapped by the single story.

Adichie herself admits she fell into that trap during a trip to Mexico. "I realized that I had been so immersed in the media coverage of Mexicans that they had become one thing in my mind, the abject immigrant. I had bought into the single story of Mexicans, and I could not have been more ashamed of myself. So that is how to create a single story. Show a people as one thing, as only one thing, over and over again, and that is what they become."

Here's a "single story" from our Amazon days. There was a large manufacturing company in the Seattle area that had the reputation for being slow and bureaucratic. (The danger of a single story applies just as easily to companies as it does to people.) We were in a hiring-decision meeting discussing a candidate from this company. Amazon sees itself as a flat organization that is anything but bureaucratic, so the single story of this manufacturing company played a significant role in the discussion. Although this candidate met every criterion and presented as an excellent hire, one leader expressed strong reservations. He felt that this person would not be successful since a previous hire he knew of from this company struggled with the speed and intensity of Amazon. He had a single story about the manufacturing company and the one employee he encountered from there, and he projected it onto all its employees. We challenged his perspective, ultimately hiring the candidate, and in doing so dropped a pebble of open-mindedness we hoped would cause a ripple in similar situations.

In the same way that you are looking to expand your stories of individuals, you should look to expand your stories of your competitors and other companies, especially those from whom you attract potential candidates. To paraphrase Adichie, it's not that the stereotype drawn from the single story is wrong—in the case of the first employee, it wasn't—it's that it's incomplete. It simply isn't the whole picture.

Getting to know your people goes a long way toward challenging single stories and driving connection and trust. But how can you support your team members in building individual connections with one another? How can you build inclusive teams which share that vision of a culture of belonging, a place where every individual supports and values every other individual?

It starts at the beginning: recruitment. Building a culture of belonging depends on leaders selecting people for the team who value inclusion and belonging. Who prioritize "we" over "me" and team wins over individual glory. Who share their experience and knowledge and help team members avoid mistakes. Who learn from mistakes when they occur.

But let's acknowledge that there's a big difference between having shared values of inclusion and living those values. When tensions are high, when leaders are under work stress, when personal ambition and financial goals intersect, leaders, like all humans, can become more insular, prioritizing their own needs. Their values can suffer. This is why leaders must model behaviors of inclusion so that the expectation is continually reinforced among all team members. This is why leaders are key to the daily practices of inclusion.

As a leader, you are a role model, and your people are watching and hearing you all the time—your voice, your body language, your eye contact, your tone, and the words you choose—whether in the hallway, on Zoom, in one-on-one meetings, in staff meetings, or in your emails. If you spend time with kids, you know they're watching your actions as much as or more than your words. They see everything—all your conscious and unconscious behaviors. They see you. The same goes for your team members.

Through your daily actions and behaviors, you either build up or tear down the trust and confidence of your team. When trust and confidence in you are high, you have created the psychological safety that helps build a culture where people take risks and openly share their ideas and perspectives—even when they are the lone dissenter "speaking truth to power." But without that trust and psychological safety, team members aren't going to show up authentically. They won't feel that they belong. And they certainly won't share their differing perspectives, which may be the ones the team needs to hear the most.

We all have a natural bias toward people like ourselves. We've been taught since we were children that what is different is dangerous and what is similar is safe. As adults, however, we need to acknowledge that what is different makes us stronger and what is similar makes us duplicative.

But it's difficult to feel you belong when you're the only one. If you're the only Black woman, the only transgender team member, or the only employee with a disability in the group, you are less likely to feel a connection to teammates. Being the only one is such a common dynamic for historically underestimated, marginalized, or oppressed people that there's a name for it: onliness.

When there is one person in the room with a different way of looking at the problem, or they are the one person of color, or the one woman, or the only person with some other dimension of diversity, listen to them. They deserve to be seen, heard, supported, and understood. A culture of belonging is one in which everyone feels safe to be the only one who looks like them or who has had their experiences. A culture of belonging also welcomes individuals who have an opinion on the margins or who are perhaps the lone voice of dissent. They too need to be heard and supported, and their perspectives considered. And they may be right. Every opinion counts.

Leaders need every person's perspective and creativity to address and solve the difficult, complex problems facing your organization.

Leaders need to build a culture where people in the room physically lean in and truly listen to those only voices. That's when innovation happens. That's when inclusion and belonging pay dividends.

The daily practices of inclusion are becoming exceedingly crucial to leadership success as workplaces become increasingly diverse. Leaders are hiring people who come from all over the world. We're all working with people of every culture, faith, ethnicity, physical or mental ability, gender expression, immigration status, sexual orientation, race, language, size, military status, and geographic location, and every intersectionality. Effective diverse teams lean heavily on leaders' understanding and modeling how to navigate the barriers that prevent people of different backgrounds and life experiences from maximizing their contributions.

## ARE WE THERE YET?

As you travel on your Inclusive Leadership journey, you're going to want to know: Are we there yet? How do I measure progress toward a culture of belonging? How do I measure inclusion? How do I know when we're "there"?

Certainly, we utilize engagement surveys, ID&E maturity assessments, and other quantitative data such as workforce demographics and hiring, promotion, and retention rates. In aggregate these data tell a story and helps us understand the gaps between where an organization is today and their aspirational future state.

But perhaps the most comprehensive measure of inclusion and belonging comes from connecting directly with the most vulnerable people in your organization, those folks who have the experience of being the only one. Qualitative data from focus groups, one-to-one meetings, informal dialogue, and conversations are incredibly useful for gaining an understanding of people's lived experience. In these conversations, you need to listen to understand with heart, with deep empathy. To lead with your ears.

The practices you'll learn here will help build a culture of belonging that benefits your most vulnerable employees—and everyone else too. Everyone benefits from the daily practices because Inclusive Leadership is about leading all people. We all share a desire to be seen, heard, valued, and understood. We all have an innate desire to be included and to feel we belong. And we need to have everyone in the boat with all their perspectives to succeed in reaching whatever goals we set.

# Chapter 2

# DAILY WISDOM

*Seven Insights for Leading Inclusively*

## Pam Maynard on the Human Connection

Pam Maynard is currently the CEO at Avanade, the leading global provider of digital, cloud, AI, advisory services, industry solutions, and design-led experiences across the Microsoft ecosystem.

For Pam, feeling safe is a consistent inclusion theme and, in her mind, an outcome generated when leaders care about the people around them. She believes that leaders must know their people as humans and that the vulnerability to listen and acknowledge what you don't know is a defining characteristic of Inclusive Leadership.

In her own words:

> *I think it is all too easy when you are a leader in a big services business like ours to get fixated on the employee numbers—the numbers of people that you have and getting them chargeable and understanding their payroll costs and how that is increasing versus revenue. But for me, Inclusive Leadership isn't about understanding how*

*many employees you have; it actually is about learning and understanding who people are. Which is why I spend a lot of time just hosting, getting out there talking to people, round tables, having reverse mentoring calls, learning what is helpful for our people and not helpful for our people. Because without that how do you know what they need in order for them to feel like they can belong and what they need from you as a leader, right?*

*We learned through our ally survey that our Black women in the US were suffering. They didn't feel engaged. They didn't feel well. They didn't feel that their careers were progressing at Avanade. So we put in place a deliberate intervention that we called Sisters Unfiltered, which was our group in the US, and it was brilliant, actually. Sisters Unfiltered is a purposefully organized group of Black women who are there to ensure we don't overlook their lived experiences and, in fact, see them. We still run it now and come together probably three times a year with me as well to listen.*

*But the fact that I'm not an African American ... what right did I have to bring this group of women together? And how would they feel about it? [Pam is Black and English].*

*It took courage, vulnerability, and compassion to say, "Look, I haven't walked in your shoes. I absolutely acknowledge that. I've lived in the US and I've observed some bits, and I've also observed how I've been treated, before people knew that I was English, right?"*

*I said to them that I acknowledge, and I've seen that your experience is not what I would want for you in Avanade. So I'm here to learn and I'm here to listen. I'm here to do whatever I can to help. That is a different type of courage I had to show, but it was absolutely the right thing to do.*

*I go back to the pandemic days . . . I actually think that was a great opportunity for us to really learn who our people were and the circumstances of their lives. You know, who they were as humans. Like when I was having a conversation with someone and his daughters were jumping up and down on the bed behind him because his office—his makeshift office—was his bedroom and his two daughters were having a good old time behind him. It was hilarious.*

When our now-adult kids were growing up, we made sure to share the important difference between being book smart and street smart. We were as focused on how they were learning to navigate the everyday challenges of life, socially, culturally, and politically, as we were on their learning in the classroom.

Leaders must also evolve their knowledge and intelligence (book smarts) into wisdom (street smarts). It is far more difficult to *be* an inclusive leader than it is to *understand the qualities* of inclusive leaders. It's one thing to think about Inclusive Leadership; it's another thing to do it. And the only way to get good at it is to do it every day—hence the importance of daily practices.

Developing the wisdom to lead a diverse workforce is a challenge that exists today for many leaders. Wisdom is a muscle that requires daily exercise to grow and strengthen. It requires a lifelong commitment to doing the work of learning about and understanding people and cultures, customs, norms, and styles.

We developed the Insights of Inclusive Leadership (2IL) model to help you do this work. Intelligence is understanding what the seven insights are. Wisdom will come from learning how to apply them in your daily life as a leader to build a culture of belonging.

## THINKING LIKE AN INCLUSIVE LEADER

There are many, many ways to characterize Inclusive Leadership. If you are curious, type "inclusive leadership definition" into your favorite search engine and look at the flood of hits you get. Our Insights of Inclusive Leadership (2IL) model, illustrated in figure 2.1, is a very comprehensive and easy to understand one that illuminates all the key insights and concepts you should think through as you develop your Inclusive Leadership wisdom.

As our work and the field of ID&E evolved, we realized we needed a framework in order to hold legitimate, impactful conversations about the key drivers of Inclusive Leadership. It was important to name the daily dynamics that were driving inclusive interactions and engagement. Developing the model facilitated dialogue and understanding, and helped grow leaders' awareness of their impacts on others, especially when unintentional.

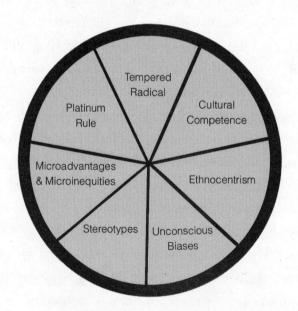

Figure 2.1. Insights of Inclusive Leadership model

The 2IL model is rooted in social psychological principles addressing how

- Individuals interact one-to-one, one-to-a few, and one-to-many
- People function day-in and day-out given all of the external, often unconscious stimuli bombarding them constantly
- In-group/out-group dynamics play out
- People perceive their identity and how this perception affects their interactions with others
- Oppression, racism, antisemitism, sexism, and other forms of discrimination manifest during interactions

Social psychological perspectives help you understand why, for example, what someone intends has the opposite impact, why leaders build teams made up of people who look and behave like everyone else on the team, and why the same people are consistently promoted or given visibility to leadership. The list could go on, but you get the point.

The 2IL model is also built on a shared understanding of diversity, inclusion, equity, and intersectionality. A shared understanding helps in creating a common vision for why this work is needed and how best to approach it. Without it, there could be a critical misalignment of the why and how of ID&E strategies and programs. The following sections briefly describe these key terms. For a more in-depth look at these and other important ID&E concepts, scan the following QR code with your phone for an exclusive video discussion of this topic. In the video, we also address misconceptions about the impact ID&E has on majority populations, such as white people, men, people without disabilities, nonveterans, and so on.

## Diversity

We like to envision diversity as a tree with a robust root. The various dimensions of diversity are either visible (in the branches and leaves of the tree) or invisible (in the root system below ground). (See figure 2.2; the diversity tree shown here represents one possible combination of visible and invisible dimensions, but is in no way an exhaustive list or necessarily globally contextual.)

We might characterize race as a visible dimension of diversity, whereas thinking style may fit as an invisible dimension. It is important to note, however, that what may be a visible aspect of diversity for one person may be an invisible one for another. Race can be invisible,

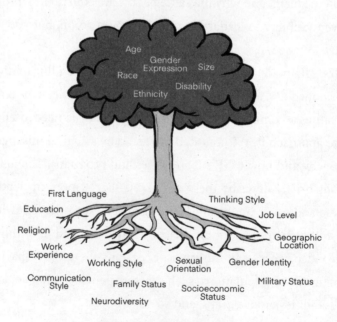

**Figure 2.2. Diversity tree**

as some people can be perceived as being of another race or actively "pass" for another race. Having a disability is another great example. Someone in a wheelchair has a visible dimension of diversity. However, for someone who is dyslexic or with a very tiny hearing aid, their dimensions of diversity may be invisible.

## Inclusion

If diversity is what comes through your doors, inclusion is what you do with it—how you ensure that each person with their visible and invisible dimensions of diversity feels seen and valued, and that they belong. There is obviously more context and complexity to the notion of inclusion, but this definition, for us, has been a good jump-off point for meaningful conversations.

## Equity

Equity is everyone getting what they need in order to be successful. It is about ensuring that systems, practices, mechanisms, and policies provide equal access to the opportunities, recognition, and resources that support success. Equity is *not* about creating undue advantage or disadvantage for anyone. It is about fairness.

## Intersectionality

According to Catalyst, a leading think tank with a mission of accelerating progress for women through workplace inclusion, "Intersectionality is a framework for understanding how social identities—such as gender, race, ethnicity, social class, religion, sexual orientation, ability, and gender identity—overlap with one another and with systems of power that oppress and advantage people in the workplace and broader community."[1] A critical aspect of what Catalyst is saying is that it isn't enough to simply add up all of a person's perceived aspects of identity. When you look at how people's identities intersect, you should see their unique lived experiences through the lens of privilege, oppression, power, and marginalization.

The term *intersectionality* was coined by UCLA Distinguished Professor of Law and civil rights activist Kimberlé Crenshaw in 1989 to make the point that not all women share or experience the same levels of discrimination simply because they are women. She contended that antiracist politics, antidiscrimination, and feminist theory failed to recognize the lived experiences of Black women like herself because these perspectives focused solely on one diversity dimension: gender. We saw this clearly illustrated in one of our previous companies. An empirical analysis of attrition data showed a significant attrition rate for women that was much higher than that of their male coworkers. When we looked at the intersection of race and gender, however, we found an astonishing insight in those data sets: attrition wasn't an issue for all women. As it turns out, the attrition rate of Black women was three to four times higher than that of Latine and Asian women and five times that of white women. A simplistic one-dimensional view of diversity masked the true issue. Armed with this knowledge, we were able to intentionally zero in on closing the Black women's attrition gap, using far fewer resources to do so.

## Empathy, Inclusion, and Belonging

The notion of belonging is fundamentally human. It is more than wanting to belong to something. According to Amanda Enayati, "As humans, we *need* to belong. To one another, to our friends and families, to our culture and country, to our world. Belonging is primal, fundamental to our sense of happiness and well-being."[2]

The pathway from inclusion to belonging is an important one. Inclusion is the means; belonging is the end. Leaders build a culture of belonging by being inclusive, by dropping pebbles of inclusion daily that cause ripples of change throughout their organizations.

We will discuss empathy in depth in chapter 4, but it is important to lay the groundwork here. In their essay, "Empathy: The First Step towards Inclusion," Adetoun Yeaman and Sreyoshi Bhaduri state: "Empathy is the gateway to inclusion because it makes us aware of our privileges, as well as the inequality of opportunities and resources, the denial of human rights that plagues a huge portion of the population in the world."[3] Yeaman and Bhaduri draw an important distinction between feeling someone's pain and understanding it. You can't feel someone else's pain, because it has not been your experience, they write, "But you can have respect, interest, and curiosity to listen and understand the stories and realities of people who walked different paths from yours. When you know and understand all the barriers, challenges, exclusions, and prejudices faced by someone, you begin to empathize with that person." Empathy is necessary for Inclusive Leadership, and Inclusive Leadership is what builds a culture of belonging. Each of the seven insights of Inclusive Leadership—cultural competence, ethnocentrism, unconscious bias, stereotyping, microadvantages and microinequities, the Platinum Rule, and being a tempered radical—require leaders to have empathy for the people around them.

## THE SEVEN INSIGHTS OF INCLUSIVE LEADERSHIP

In this section, we'll explore each insight and how you can evolve your knowledge of what it means into wisdom you can hone in your daily life. Each insight by itself has an impact; however, it's critical to also consider how they relate to one another. For example, a lack of cultural competence can impact how ethnocentric a leader is, which may be driven by an unquestioned stereotype they've had about a particular group of people, and so on. A big part of developing the wisdom to lead inclusively is making these insights your own and being real with yourself about how they have influenced you personally and how they intersect in your daily life.

## Cultural Competence

**Cultural competence** (figure 2.3) is an experiential understanding and acceptance of the beliefs, values, and ethics of others as well as the demonstrated skills necessary to work with and serve diverse individuals and groups.

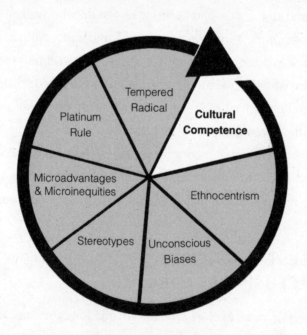

Figure 2.3. Insights of Inclusive Leadership model:
Cultural competence

Developing cultural competence is a dynamic process requiring ongoing self-assessment and continual expansion of your cultural knowledge about and respect for others. It begins with an understanding of your own culture, continues through interactions with individuals from various cultures, and extends through your expansion of knowledge. As you might have guessed, a prerequisite for cultural competence is a desire to learn about difference and how others' differences align with who they are. You must want to learn about stuff outside your own limits, culture, and norms. Building cultural competency occurs over time, and as it develops, so too does the ability to see cultural differences not as a problem but a strength.

You develop cultural competence through interactions with people and groups that are different from you. This is a basic but key starting point. To become culturally competent, you need to actually experience difference, to venture into new territory, to step away from the comfortable into the unknown. It involves finding multiple ways to learn about different cultures—from books and food to conversation and travel, and more. Becoming culturally competent is a lifelong pursuit—and what a fun pursuit at that! None of us are ever done with developing cultural competence.

In recent years, the term *cultural humility* has become more prevalent in discussions surrounding cultural competence. We continue to use "cultural competence," as we believe that cultural humility—being respectfully curious about other people and cultures without assuming you know it all—is a part of this critical concept, not simply a different name for it.

This journey of cultural competency can begin with self-learning (e.g., using books, movies, videos, and podcasts), but experiencing difference in real life is the most impactful and arguably the most fun way to grow this skill. Traveling is clearly a great way to learn about other cultures, but your "trip" doesn't always have to be out of your area or country. Don't get us wrong: if you have the resources to do so, traveling abroad and experiencing different cultures, environments, and geographies are an amazing way to develop cultural competency skills. But that's not the only way, and it sets a high bar. Try traveling to areas that you know are different from your own where there are folks from different cultures or life experiences. Developing cultural competence can be as easy as finding authentic "ethnic" restaurants near you and experiencing the food and atmosphere, and, if you are comfortable doing so, engaging with the folks around you.

Join organizations in which you would be considered an ally or accomplice of that group. Show that you have an interest in the group and value it enough to want to be a part of it, to respectfully learn from its members, and to do your part to help them with the challenges they face.

There are many rich resources to help you learn how to respectfully interact with people from other cultures. Classic studies and books teach about the different dimensions of culture. We like Fons Trompenaars and Charles Hampden-Turner's highly consumable *Riding the Waves of Culture* and Geert Hofstede's influential book *Cultures and Organizations: Software of the Mind*. There are more recent books on the topic, such as Erin Meyer's *The Culture Map: Breaking through the Invisible Boundaries of Global Business*, which does an outstanding job of providing very useful anecdotes and stories to help you understand and apply the lessons of cultural styles to your work across the globe. There are also many assessment tools available such as Aperian's GlobeSmart, Erin Meyer's Culture Mapping Tool, Hofstede's Country Comparison Tool, and the assessment framework from the Cultural Intelligence Center. We've used GlobeSmart for over twenty-five years, and we particularly like it because it's a great source of cultural information that is interactive and graphically engaging, and uses multiple learning methods. Whatever your mode of learning, the key is to be willing to ask questions and truly listen. That is how you develop the wisdom that will help you on your journey.

Here are a few examples of when a lack of cultural competence had far-reaching effects. Before launching Microsoft's Zune, a planned iPod competitor in Israel, it would have been good to know that *Zune* sounds like a vulgarity in Hebrew.[4] The company also lost millions in software sales due to incorrectly or insensitively color-coding maps of world time zones. For one, the disputed Jammu-Kashmir region was not shown as a part of India—an offense under Indian law. For a short time, the software was banned in the country because of this transgression. Second, a software map showed Kurdistan to be a separate entity from Turkey, which led to the arrest of Microsoft employees in Turkey. Third, the company somehow managed to depict the Korean flag backward.[5] These examples make the business case for leaders to grow cultural competence daily. Even if an inclusive leader was not aware of the cultural issues around mapping the world, they would at least have had the cultural competence to ask the questions.

We encourage leaders and all employees to "think global, act local." Throughout your work as a people leader or individual contributor, evaluate your personal behavior, the decisions you consider, and your work product through a global lens. Consider the impact of everything you do on how it will be received by people and cultures around the world. Likewise, ID&E strategy should be globally inclusive; you can accomplish this by working closely with local market experts to develop specific solutions based on local market challenges, opportunities, and issues, whether that be in the US, India, Japan, Israel, Brazil, or Germany. It is also important to listen closely to employees in local markets and empower them to take ownership of the work.

## Ethnocentrism

**Ethnocentrism** (figure 2.4) is our human tendency to judge another culture or individual by the values and standards of our own culture, particularly with regard to language, behavior, customs, and religion.

There is a problem if a person believes that only their culture makes sense, has the right values, or represents the only logical way to behave. This is true also for how someone thinks about the companies they work for and compete with. They can feel very strongly that their company does things the right way and other companies are simply not as good, when really those companies are just different.

Interestingly, not all ethnocentrism is bad. In fact, there are two forms of ethnocentrism: mild and wild. Yes, those are the sociological terms! A mild form of ethnocentrism leads to in-group cohesion and

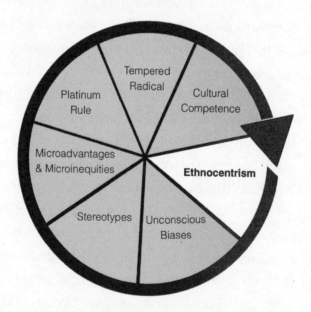

Figure 2.4. Insights of Inclusive Leadership model: Ethnocentrism

solidarity. For example, wearing a shirt that says, "Unapologetically BLACK and Proud" is mild ethnocentrism which expresses that you like being Black or African American. The same can be said for wearing any company-branded shirt. Wild ethnocentrism, by contrast, leads to feelings of arrogance or disdain for others and is clearly a barrier to leading inclusively. In other words, wild ethnocentrism is in play when someone allows their belief in the superiority of their cultural perspective to negatively influence how they lead, interview, handle conflict, give guidance, or work with people from other cultures.

Leading inclusively may involve mild forms of ethnocentrism. It is perfectly good to admire your culture, teams, or company. However, allowing wild forms of ethnocentrism to drive your engagements will seriously reduce your ability to leverage different perspectives, cultures, and experiences as well as create the ripple effect of change that leads to a culture of belonging.

An example of ethnocentrism played out for us in the first hour of an Amazon business trip to Bengaluru, India. On the car ride from the airport to the hotel, we noticed the cars and motorbikes driving all over the road, not in set lanes, and the drivers hitting their horns constantly with quick little "beep-beep, beep-beeps." The horns did not signal that the drivers were angry; they just let everyone around them know, "Here I am." Because of the sheer density of the traffic and lack of apparent respect for lines in the road, if they existed at all, cars and motorbikes were weaving everywhere! And the motorbikes often had whole families on them! Along the sides of the road were cows, bicycles, and pedestrians. We exclaimed out loud how bizarre it all was. This is problematic! This is bedlam! There are going to be accidents all over the place!

But it all worked fine. Everyone got to where they needed to go. Over the course of the weeklong trip, we did not witness one accident, yet there were so many times when we judged the behavior as wrong. That was ethnocentrism. We were judging the locals' ability to drive safely and orderly based on our understanding of what is correct and right. It wasn't that their driving was wrong; it was simply different, not what we were accustomed to experiencing. Now when we travel, we ask ourselves, "Is this truly problematic, or is it simply different?"

There are easy pebbles to drop that will interrupt the wild ethnocentric tendencies that lead to bad decisions. First, name ethnocentrism and discuss it with your team so that everyone understands what it is, how it works, and its impact. Ask others to point out when you are being wildly ethnocentric—whether in casual conversations or when making key employee life-cycle decisions. Indeed, make calling out ethnocentrism something the entire organization is comfortable with. When you legitimize this conversation, you take a big step toward creating an inclusive workplace environment and upping your Inclusive Leadership game.

The more you can slow down and question the inclusivity of your decisions, the more inclusive your decisions will be. One pebble you can drop during these times of reflection is to ask yourself, "Is [whatever behavior] truly problematic and wrong, or is it simply different?" Drop this simple pebble often enough and it will lead to amazing change in your organization.

## Unconscious Biases

**Unconscious biases** (figure 2.5) are implicit attitudes, actions, or judgments that stem from automatic processes in the mind not available to introspection. They can be present in thought processes, memory, affect, and motivation.

Two people enter the meeting room, one white man and one Black woman. You immediately shake the man's hand first, saying, "It's a pleasure to finally meet the leader of this team." The problem is that the

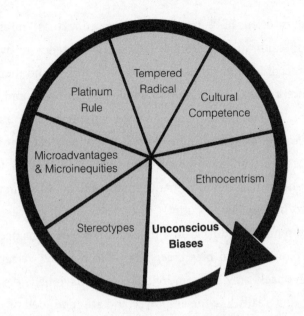

**Figure 2.5. Insights of Inclusive Leadership model: Unconscious biases**

white man isn't the leader; the Black woman is. That is unconscious bias at work. Without thought or reflection, the assumption that men are leaders and women, let alone Black women, are not has led to an embarrassing demonstration of gender and/or racial bias.

A wide variety of unconscious biases exist, and these biases creep into everything leaders do—from whom they hire, promote, fire, and assign roles to, to whom they have lunch with and create leadership visibility for. This understanding that everyone has unconscious biases has changed the way we think about and practice ID&E. We no longer point out good people versus bad people to explain racism, sexism, and other forms of discrimination. We all have biases, so there is no need to set up an Us (e.g., nonracist) versus Them (racist) dynamic. The prominence of unconscious bias as a concept in ID&E has seriously curtailed the perception that diversity work is about "outing" white men as the sole targets for change. We're all "guilty," so to speak. Here are a few examples.

Leaders often have to deal with recency bias in employee-evaluation calibration meetings. This is the tendency to overly emphasize recent actions or observations, with little or no focus on the bigger picture. Leaders ignore the whole body of work and base our evaluation only on the latest good or bad experience. Who can relate?

Confirmation bias is another great example because it is prevalent across every stage of the employee life cycle. It is the tendency for a person to seek out information that confirms what they already believe to be true. For example, in the promotion process, leaders normally request feedback on employees they are considering promoting. Confirmation bias creeps in when a leader selectively requests feedback only from individuals who have beliefs similar to theirs. If they really like the employee and are reminded of who they were at that stage of their career, they will only look for feedback that supports that contention and ardently push back against feedback that paints a negative picture. In fact, negative feedback is often swept aside as a one-off example that has no bearing on the employee's promotability. This example also shows how biases overlap: the leader may have a strong similarity bias, which could explain why they like the employee so much and are willing to ignore significant challenges the employee may have. Similarity bias here is the tendency for someone to favor people who are more like themselves. These people may look like the leader, act like the leader, be the same gender or race as the leader, or even have attended the same university as the leader did.

One final example. Women often face performance bias, which drives assumptions about women's and men's abilities. Essentially, people tend to overestimate men's performance and underestimate women's. Performance bias also shows a bias overlap: because people tend to see women as less competent than men, they tend to blame women more for mistakes while giving them less credit for their achievements. This is called attribution bias. It's important here to point out the insidious impacts of intersectionality. Certain women experience a compounded bias as a result of the intersections of their identity. Black or Indigenous women, for example, may face a much more profound performance bias than white women at the same level. Underestimated populations often face such double (and sometimes even triple or quadruple) bias situations.

Unconscious bias can be sneaky. It affects your decision-making when you least expect it. That's why we have identified particular unconscious biases associated with each stage of the employee life cycle—to make the unconscious conscious.

Let's look at the biases leaders often encounter in talent acquisition efforts such as resume reviews, candidate phone screens, the actual interview, and hiring decisions. You've got a stack of resumes to review, deciding whom to phone-screen and whom to pass on. There's a lot of work, yet you're experienced and you know what you're looking for, so you figure you'll go through the resumes while you watch the internationally franchised TV singing competition, *The Voice*. But did you know that unconscious biases are more likely to creep in when you're not paying full attention? In these circumstances, you are much more likely to select people who are similar to those you've hired in the past, maybe even similar to you. If you're looking to increase the diversity of your team, giving your full attention to the task will help slow down your decision-making and ensure a less biased approach to moving some people into the "yes" pile and others into the "no" pile.

Speaking of *The Voice*, have you ever considered why the judges have their chairs turned around so they can't see the talent when they're performing? The producers implemented a method to interrupt the judges' natural unconscious bias. By removing the visual aid, they are not able to judge the talent based on what they're wearing, what they look like, or any other visual that could trigger unconscious biases about who is worthy of winning. The producers of the show thought critically before they made that decision!

When you're looking at resumes, do you really need to see candidates' names or know their gender? Blind sifting—temporarily removing names and other triggering information from resumes to interrupt your biases—is a pebble you can drop to create a more inclusive hiring process.

There is a debate about whether we humans can ever eliminate our biases completely, but there is agreement that trying to mitigate them is key. One pebble you can drop in this effort is to take an Implicit Association Test (IAT) and encourage your team and organization to do so as well.[6] According to Project Implicit, the IAT measures the strength of associations between concepts (e.g., Black people, gay people, women, Muslims) and evaluations (e.g., good, bad) or stereotypes (e.g., athletic, clumsy, not good leaders, terrorists). Once you've taken some IAT tests, work with your organization's ID&E professionals or HR business partners to facilitate group discussions about the biases people have discovered they have. Reinforce the importance and power of open conversations by being vulnerable as a leader. The ripple effect will be that others will feel more comfortable sharing their vulnerabilities too.

This increased understanding of your biases is a pebble you can drop every day as you reflect on the interactions you have with others around you, during the interview process, while you travel, or in your day-to-day conversations and connections. For example, after taking an IAT, you may learn you have a mild bias against Muslims. Knowing this, during an interview process with someone who is clearly Muslim, review and question your decisions and engagement to make sure that being slightly biased against Muslims didn't influence your decisions.

Dropping daily pebbles of inclusion becomes significantly easier if leaders are well versed in what unconscious biases are and how they show up in the multitude of processes in the employee life cycle, and if they do the work to understand the biases they personally have. We do feel, however, that there has been too much reliance on unconscious bias training as *the* pathway to inclusive workplaces. For us, the work on unconscious biases is but one important piece of the puzzle—the other six insights from our model are equally critical in the discussion of Inclusive Leadership, inclusive workplace environments, and creating cultures of belonging.

## Stereotypes

**Stereotypes** (figure 2.6) are exaggerated beliefs and images or distorted truths about a person, a group, a company, or a culture.

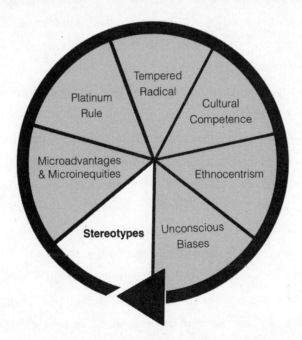

**Figure 2.6. Insights of Inclusive Leadership model: Stereotypes**

Stereotypes aren't always bad. People would not be able to function or handle the amazing amount of stimuli that we are flooded with in each given moment if we didn't stereotype. (It's the same with unconscious biases.) Think of stereotypes as overgeneralizations. If people didn't overgeneralize situations during our daily interactions, we would be bogged down trying to figure out all the individual pieces of stimuli, unable to make decisions about anything with any pace. Stereotypes help people make sense of the world by simplifying information so that it's easier to identify, recall, predict, and react to. Basically, stereotyping helps us navigate through life more quickly and easily. Similar to the danger of a single story, which we discussed in chapter 1, the problem arises when people use a stereotype to characterize a particular group, individual, or anyone else identified as "other" in a disparaging way, and interact with them accordingly. For example, all women are irrational, incapable of leading, or, in the case of Black women, angry. Or all African Americans are lazy, less intelligent, or dangerous. Or all people with disabilities are a burden. Or even, none of the people at this particular hierarchical company know how to make their own decisions.

Honestly acknowledging that you have the tendency, as all humans do, to stereotype is a key insight for leading inclusively. You evolve that knowledge into wisdom through the daily practice of questioning your decisions, actions, and statements for harmful negative generalizations, and, ultimately, changing course when you need to. The power and beauty of practicing inclusion daily is that you begin to chip away at any unchecked harmful tendencies to stereotype.

When inclusive leaders openly and vulnerably question their and others' use of stereotypes, they are dropping powerful pebbles. A daily practice for mitigating the use of negative stereotypes is simply being open to learning and actively doing so. Read an article that expands your understanding of the contributions of a group that you have stereotyped in the past. Communicate to your team and colleagues that you are doing this to be more aware and to lead more inclusively. Encourage them to do the same. These are simple daily actions that create workplace environments that are welcoming and that foster feelings of belonging.

## Microadvantages and Microinequities

**Microadvantages** (figure 2.7) are subtle actions or messages that give people a leg up or indicate they belong, simply because they are a part of the majority in-group.

**Microinequities** are subtle messages in the form of nonverbal gestures, facial expressions, messages, or body language that marginalize or exclude people based on their identity.

Oppression and exclusion, antitheses of belonging, do not require overt, in-your-face forms of malicious discrimination and harassment. Far too often, racism, antisemitism, sexism, homophobia, ableism, ageism, and so on show up in the workplace and in people's daily interactions through the subtle, sometimes unintentional things they do, say, or express nonverbally.

**Microadvantages** are subtle messages or behaviors that serve to give distinct advantages to certain people—perhaps because they remind the leader of who the leader is, they look like the leader, or they have followed a similar path in life. A microadvantage is given when you hear a leader say to their team, "I tapped Bob for this because he thinks exactly like me and attacks problems with the same take-no-prisoners approach. He is leadership material."

Interestingly, this example of a microadvantage also serves as

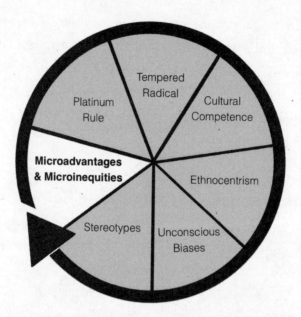

Figure 2.7. Insights of Inclusive Leadership model:
Microadvantages and microinequities

a microinvalidation or microinequity for the team members who are from marginalized groups. There is an insidious interplay between these dynamics, and understanding the exhausting impacts of microadvantages, microinequities, microaggressions, microassaults, microinvalidations, and microinsults is critical as you move through your Inclusive Leadership journey. We'll give you a sense of what each of these dynamics are, but we encourage you to research this topic more deeply. There are excellent videos and articles available free to the public. We've highlighted several in our resources section in the back of the book.

As an umbrella category, **microinequities** are focused on people without regard to their group identity. That is, anyone could be the focus of a microinequity. An example would be that a group of employees go out for coffee or drinks after work and consistently leave behind one person on the team.

**Microinsults** are subtle rude statements that demean a person's racial heritage or identity—for example, assuming a person of color is the subordinate when two people walk into the room, or commenting on how an individual is not like the others of their race or ethnicity, thinking that is a compliment. Saying "You're so pretty for a Black girl" or "You don't seem scary like other Muslims," or saying to a gay man as though it were a big surprise, "You fit right in. You seem totally straight!" is a subtle but demeaning microinsult that marginalized people face daily.

Far more insidious versions are **microaggressions**: small, speculative, but impactful insults related to someone's identity—for example, saying to a Black person, "I bet you're happy there's Affirmative Action."

**Microassaults**, according to Derald Wing Sue, a professor of counseling psychology at Columbia University, are the most explicitly violent type of microaggression. There is no subtlety to this version. Microassaults are deliberate, and there is no guesswork as to who is the target. Sue gives the examples of when a white person in a car shouts a slur at a person of color who is walking down the street, then quickly speeds away, or when a neurotypical person triggers someone's obsessive-compulsive disorder just to watch them fix the issue over and over.[7]

Finally, **microinvalidations** dismiss or minimize the thoughts, feelings, or experiential reality of someone because of their group identity. A microinvalidation occurs when someone else is given the credit for work done by a woman of color, for example, and no one speaks up to address or correct the issue.

Figure 2.8 illustrates a common microinvalidation many women face daily. We bet if we could see the faces of all the women reading this section of our book, there would be a lot of nodding!

Black and Brown people, women, and other historically marginalized individuals carry metaphorical cups that slowly accumulate with

"That's a very good suggestion,
Miss Wilson - perhaps one of the
men would like to make it?"

Figure 2.8. "That's a very good suggestion, Miss Wilson—perhaps
one of the men would like to make it?" *Source:* CartoonStock.com,
Order no. 584227. License permission. (September 2023).

microaggressions and invalidations, until they overflow, causing a profound sense of isolation, stress, anger, disengagement or even attrition. Think of the impact of these various microinequities as "death by
a thousand paper cuts." The result of this is they often feel an immense
burden while they try to work and present themselves in a way that
doesn't trigger stereotyped perceptions held by the dominant group.
Unfortunately, microinequities in all their forms often become self-ful-
filling prophesies—people conform to their stereotypes, not because
of who they are but because of who they feel forced to become.

Inclusive leaders practice daily inclusion by speaking up when
they see a microinequity impacting someone and by actively encouraging others to do the same. For example, if a man speaks over or
cuts off a woman who is speaking, an inclusive leader will stop the

conversation and redirect it. "Hold on for a second please. Tamika was speaking, and I think we all need to hear what she has to say." The impact from this pebble is validation for anyone who feels as though they don't belong. It can also have the ripple effect of empowering others to speak up when they see this dynamic taking place.

## The Platinum Rule

The **Platinum Rule** (figure 2.9): treat others how they want to be treated, not how you want to be treated.

Many of us were taught the Golden Rule growing up: treat others how we would want to be treated. With a greater understanding and respect for all the ways in which people are different, we are now challenged to consider how others want to be treated. For example, not everyone handles direct feedback well—even if that may be how you

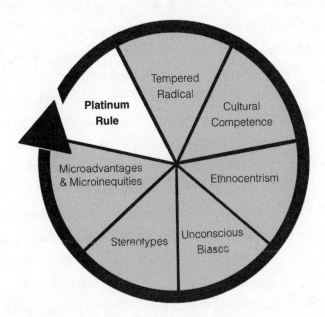

Figure 2.9. Insights of Inclusive Leadership model: The Platinum Rule

like to receive it. So you need to take a more subtle, indirect approach to helping this person improve. It does take a little more work as a leader to learn about others' preferences and act outside your normal ways of being, but it makes you more effective and inclusive. This is a good reminder that to be an inclusive leader, you need to take the time to get to know your people and truly understand who they are, what they need and why, and how they want to be led, and to understand their goals and aspirations. By centering the needs of the other person, you are showing that you really care about who they are. You aren't employing a cookie-cutter approach to interact with them, and you are taking another step toward building a culture of belonging.

Santiago Rodriguez was the director of diversity for Microsoft when Eddie joined the company in 2000. One of Santiago's leaders was a Black woman whom he valued immensely, and he wanted to reward her for her leadership and her work. In his mind, the best way to reward her was to give her spot cash bonuses and stock grants—because that's what he would love. So Santiago gave her a large stock grant and a 20K spot bonus. His intention was to show her how much he valued her. But Santiago noticed that her demeanor soon changed. She was quieter and more disengaged, perhaps even unappreciative. This baffled him. He became angry, and finally approached her about it.

"I've noticed you seem different, less engaged and upset about something. I've shown you how much I think of you as a leader and have rewarded you exactly how I would have loved to be rewarded. I've given you stock and cash; I don't understand."

What she said to him in that moment was a reminder that even people who live to do diversity work can make mistakes.

> You might like to get stock and cash rewards, but that isn't what I would want. I have plenty of stock, and I have cash. You've never once asked me how I would

like to be rewarded for all of the work and effort I put
into this team.

Santiago, all I've ever wanted you to do is recognize me and my value to your leadership team and
our mission. In front of my team, with me standing
right next to you, tell my team how much you value
me. That is what is important to me, not financial rewards. What really matters to me is that you show my
team your respect for me.

All Santiago had needed to do was to follow the Platinum Rule.
He should have asked the leader how she wanted to be appreciated—a
small, easy pebble to drop. And when she told him, the next pebble to
drop would have been clear: publicly praise her and show his appreciation for her contributions. These simple pebbles would have had an
outsized impact on how she felt about her place in the organization,
on her sense of belonging.

## Tempered Radical

A **tempered radical** (figure 2.10) understands that systemic
change requires the aggregation of a bunch of little wins that add
up to the organizational and cultural change they are seeking.

The term *tempered radical* was coined by Debra Meyerson in her
book of the same name, which has since been retitled *Rocking the
Boat*. A tempered radical knows that they don't have to do it all and
certainly not all at once. For us, being a tempered radical means that
leaders don't need to do it all or overwhelm themselves by adding
tons of ID&E stuff to their already full plates. Just do one thing. Find
a pebble each day and drop it. It could be as simple as respectfully

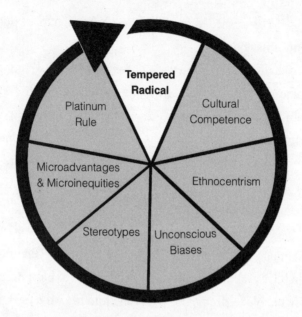

Figure 2.10. Insights of Inclusive Leadership model: Tempered radical

calling someone out (or in) in a meeting for unintentionally using a microinvalidation. It could be adding an ID&E participation question to a promotion process or discussing an unconscious bias terminology priming or reminder document before every talent-review process. Priming is a useful technique to interrupt potential bias. Have your interviewers read the required skills and abilities in a job description just prior to interviewing job candidates. By doing so, they are more inclined to focus on the objective requirements rather than subjective influences. This technique can be applied to promotion decisions, performance ratings, and any decision-making in the employment life cycle. It can also be used by introducing the use of a "pause button" to slow a conversation down so that an intentional or unintentional ID&E-related issue can be addressed without causing too much undue stress (see chapter 8).

Do small things consistently. Develop a daily practice of dropping pebbles. This tempered approach gives you a means of operationalizing your inclusion efforts in a way that doesn't become all-consuming and hence unrealistic.

A story about our partnership with Ryan Brown, now VP of Environment, Health, and Safety (EHS) and Environmental, Social, and Governance (ESG) at Coupang in South Korea, is a good illustration. When Ryan was an Amazon EHS director, he worked with us to implement candidate slating into the hiring process for his team even though the larger divisional organization was not on board. Candidate slating for us meant that for every open position, we had to interview at least two women and/or people of color. The upstream ripple effect on talent acquisition was that recruiters had to cast a wider net. As a result, they discovered rich new resources of talent in professional and technical organizations focused on women and people of color, as well as in historically Black colleges and universities and Hispanic-serving institutions. They also identified new Boolean search techniques to identify alumni from Black and Brown fraternities and sororities. Candidate slating resulted in a significant increase in the representation of historically underrepresented people on the team. Ryan took a risk by dropping a pebble that rocked the boat at Amazon, leading the way as a tempered radical.

## CULTIVATING DAILY WISDOM

The 2IL model is an important framework to guide your growth as a leader. It gives you a common language and understanding that facilitates meaningful engagement. It gives you a means by which to challenge others to adopt and intentionally deploy insights, tools, and mechanisms that create inclusive workplace environments and build cultures of belonging.

This deep ID&E work takes time and will stretch and challenge you. When you do the personal work to integrate these critical insights into your daily practices, you enable a more robust, impactful, and fulfilling Inclusive Leadership journey.

We encourage you to own as much of the ID&E topic as you can and commit to a continuous learning journey; this is how you develop the wisdom to drop pebbles strategically. Part of that ongoing journey is also growing your awareness of the behavioral and conceptual dynamics that undergird your actions and behavior. These include having the courage to act and the heart to demonstrate empathy, compassion, and vulnerability. For example, there will be times when you need to rock the boat hard enough to knock people, and potentially yourself, out of the boat. Leaders need the wisdom to know when such a move is necessary, *and* they need the courage to do it. That courage is the focus of the next chapter.

Chapter 3

# DAILY COURAGE

*A Willingness to Rock the Boat*

## Sean Kelley on Rocking the Boat

Sean Kelley was the head of talent acquisition (TA) for Worldwide Operations at Amazon. He is currently retired from corporate life but continues to have an impact as the founder of Sage & Sea Ventures, where he advises on talent acquisition and military veteran success. When we asked Sean to talk about Inclusive Leadership, he told a series of illuminating stories that capture an important foundation of Inclusive Leadership: the courage to rock the boat.

Sean described how he rocked the boat with intentionality during his first meeting as the leader of TA at Amazon when it was clear that diversity metrics weren't being considered in talent reviews.

> *I set the tone by saying, I'm here as an observer, but next year this isn't how this will go. If you are really low on your diversity metrics, you are going to be really low on your performance outcomes. I explained to the team that diversity may not have been a priority, so at all-hands meetings, I*

*will always have someone report out on diversity—a project, a win, a struggle, and eventually from around the world. To just be intentional about it.*

He also told the story of engaging his peers with intentional questions at a performance review meeting.

*It was me and my peers, all the senior leaders, and when they went through their first wave of succession planning, all the top-ranked HR people were dudes [men]. I said, "Okay, 75 percent women in HR and hey, I'm curious if anyone else noticed, but we have not identified any women leaders. I don't see us doing a great job, collectively, of identifying future leaders who are women for a majority-women org."*

Sean is an expert in calling people in by using curious questions so they don't become defensive and they actually seek to understand and learn instead of shutting down. It's part of his courageous Inclusive Leadership. (For more on calling in versus calling out, see chapter 8.)

*You have to ask the question without punching them in the nose, but also not be afraid to ask it. As an inclusive leader, you have to point out things when it seems like we are missing the mark.*

The last story Sean told involved coauthor Eddie, when they worked together at Microsoft, and it exemplifies how inclusive leaders have the courage to always be learning.

*When I first started working with you [Eddie] on the diversity team, being LGBTQ was very foreign to me. So I went to a Northwest Diversity Learning series event, and I brought a couple of my straight, white leaders from my team. I invited people to go into an uncomfortable learning environment to point out that we all have to under-*

> stand it, to learn to talk about it, and align our hearts and
> our heads on a topic that we just haven't experienced in
> our lives.
>
> Later on, Sean's daughter came out as gay, which made
> him extra glad that he had done that work.
>
> *In hindsight, I was prepping myself to be a more inclusive
> dad. I was sure my heart and head had settled any incon-
> sistencies from what I learned from growing up.*

Inclusive leaders need courage because it's hard to keep chipping away at entrenched cultural norms. It takes a long time for ID&E efforts to see results, and there is usually a lot of accompanying disruption to contend with. ID&E work kicks up dust; for you and others, it might feel like things are getting worse before they get better. There is also the reality that leaders often get only one shot to do ID&E work. If it fails—for any reason—there is little will to invest in trying again.

Leaders at all levels are compelled to deliver big results and to do so creatively and effectively. They make a name for themselves because they are intentional about doing the hard work—even if it means sometimes straying from the beaten path. Intentionality, in the context of ID&E work, is knowing when to rock the boat and rock it hard to see your strategic imperatives come to life. Leaders realize that you don't have to do it all by themselves or with a massive undertaking that eats up lots of their limited bandwidth. It is dropping strategic pebbles of inclusion—every day—that lead to ripples of change.

Business executives always ask us, "What are the three big things I can do to integrate ID&E into my organization? You know, the big-impact, big-splash things?" But big, splashy, one-off actions are not how sustainable change happens in the ID&E space. The best way for leaders, at all levels, to effect change is through the aggregation of consistent daily actions, tactics, and behaviors that add up to sustainable systemic and organizational change. This tempered radical approach takes courage.

Think of your organization as the boat. All the employees are in the boat, and the boat is surrounded by water that represents your organizational culture. As we've said, when you, the leader, drop a pebble of inclusion into the water, it creates a ripple in the culture. This causes other employees to drop pebbles, which creates a larger ripple effect. And so on. Eventually the ripples become a wave of systemic cultural change that rocks the boat. If the wave is strong enough, it might even knock some employees out of the boat.

To be an inclusive leader, you need to have the wisdom to know what pebbles lead to rocking the boat, and the courage to drop those pebbles on a daily basis. The good thing is that you only need the courage to keep dropping pebbles—the ripple effect and boat-rocking will take care of themselves.

## HOW HARD IS TOO HARD?

An inclusive leader is someone who is willing to rock the boat hard but—ideally—not so hard that you rock anyone out of the boat. For the most part, you need everyone in the boat to make or inspire systemic and organizational change. For the most part. Sometimes, however, as we mentioned earlier, it is necessary to rock the boat hard enough to knock certain people, even potentially yourself, out of the boat.

We came to this important realization during a discussion at the National Association of African Americans in Human Resources conference back in the early 2000s. We were pressed to expand our thinking and acknowledge that there will be times when knocking people out of the boat or even capsizing the entire boat is absolutely legitimate and necessary. When someone does something so egregious and inappropriate that their very presence is poisoning the culture of the organization, it may well be the right thing to knock them out of the boat. Further, there may be people or organizations that are so intolerable, so toxic that the best thing you can do for yourself is to knock yourself out of the boat—or even capsize it! Here is Eddie's real-life example to illustrate this point.

> At one of my previous companies, a senior executive in charge of running much of the European business made a comment about people's physical size that was egregious and explicitly inappropriate. The ID&E trainer indicated that people who are obese often face discrimination in the workplace, to which the senior executive very matter-of-factly replied: "I wouldn't ever hire fat people because they are lazy, undisciplined, and make horrible employees."
>
> The impact of this blatantly discriminatory statement was instant and toxic. The trainer, a junior-level manager, and the other participants were shocked. The trainer explained to us later that it was very hard to continue the training and that the senior executive's vicious stereotyping shut down a lot of the conversation in the room going forward.
>
> Not surprisingly, investigating the situation unearthed other inappropriate sexist and xenophobic comments from the senior exec. Another leader and I decided to capsize the boat on this one and risk getting knocked out ourselves. We immediately confronted

the leader, discussed the situation with his boss, and requested that meaningful action be taken. We also circled back with the trainer to acknowledge the impact the exec's words had and to let her know that we took action. It took a year of rocking the boat, but eventually the leader was removed from the company.

In conclusion, although there's no blanket answer for how hard to rock the boat, our suggestion is to channel deceased US congressman and civil rights activist John Lewis: rock it hard enough to "make good trouble."

## THE COURAGE TO DROP A PEBBLE

Inclusive leaders work toward transformational ends through incremental means. Whether it's by resisting quietly, leveraging small wins, or mobilizing others in legitimate but powerful ways, they build the courage to keep going. Yes, inclusive leaders need the intentionality and willingness to rock the boat, but on a daily basis, all they need is the courage to drop a pebble.

There is a reason we highlighted Sean Kelley as one of our inclusive leaders. He has lived his career rocking boats—intentionally, and on occasion unintentionally—with genuine courage and always with an ID&E lens filtering the work he does. As we spoke with Sean, another story popped up that will give you an even better sense of what a wise and courageous inclusive leader looks like.

Sean moved from doing ID&E work on Microsoft's Central Diversity team to Microsoft's Talent Acquisition team in 2008. His remit was to recruit for the human resources, legal, and finance organizations. One of his responsibilities was to hire lawyers and help the general counsel (GC) staff up his organization. Sean began by asking the question, Does where a lawyer went to school have any correlation with performance and performance scores at Microsoft? He and his team wanted to create a more diverse pool of lawyers, and they wondered what would happen if their search was not limited to certain prestige schools, which were by nature less racially diverse.

The assessment revealed that where a lawyer went to school mattered very little. The results made it clear that if they were going to find more diverse talent and win in the market, they needed to look for the top 10 percent of students from any school and not just from the top five to ten schools.

Sean let a close advisor to the GC know that they were going to change the profile of places to source lawyer talent. In addition to widening the field of potential candidates, his strategy was to create a shared responsibility with the GC for integrating an ID&E perspective into sourcing. Sean was rocking the boat.

The GC had a big, negative reaction to this new strategy. But Sean remained strong in his conviction. This approach was not only the right thing to do but also made excellent business sense. Instead of backing away, he brought his information, his analysis, and his courage to his discussions with the GC.

"Hey, not everyone who goes to Harvard will come to Microsoft and be successful," he respectfully argued. It was hard to refute Sean's well-researched analysis and deny his passion. The GC walked back his reservations and eventually became a very willing partner.

Sean had the foresight to drop a pebble—ask if there was a better way to recruit diverse talent—and the courage to rock the boat once he realized the answer was yes. The massive ripple effect was the systemic change in how Microsoft sourced lawyer talent. Sean's efforts had a sustained impact on the recruitment approach, and, ultimately, the racial and gender demographics of the staff. Not surprisingly, the innovation and creativity of the legal team also increased.

Probably the most significant impact Sean had was getting senior leadership to challenge the misguided perception that there wasn't Black and Brown talent in the legal field to be found. He was able to drop the pebble that illuminated the best way to find diverse talent: fish where they are.

Sean's story highlights several daily practices of inclusion that had systemic and organizational impacts. First, he and his team widened, and therefore diversified, the recruitment pool. Then they implemented a diverse candidate slating requirement, meaning that a search could not be closed until at least two women and/or people of color were interviewed. This caused multiple ripples throughout the organization. If people wanted to move on a single-person loop and make an offer without candidate slating, they had to have permission in writing from their GC to do so. The result was that they had to slow down and really consider why they wanted to bypass the requirement. The slating requirement not only directly increased the diversity of candidates interviewed and hired but also helped people shift their thinking around culture fit versus culture add.

The team realized that hiring for culture fit is reactive and leads to more of the status quo, more conformity, and ultimately stagnation. It replicates what is already in place without stretching the team's ability to meet new, growing, and diverse challenges. The team learned that hiring for culture add, on the other hand, is proactive and leads to innovation, growth, and diversity.

Sean's efforts not only reshaped the profile of what a Microsoft lawyer looks like—in reality and in the minds of leaders—but also forced longer-term thinking about how the organization engages with and curates relationships with professional organizations, such as the

Hispanic National Bar Association, the National Society of Black Engineers, and the Society of Women Engineers. Microsoft's engagement with these and other organizations became more direct and felt more like forming partnerships as a result of this effort.

One final, significant ripple from this story: the GC became a champion of these inclusive efforts and intentionally moved sourcing and hiring data and analysis from the appendix section of a critical recurrent report to the primary PowerPoint deck, where it would actually be reviewed. This sent a message from one of the most powerful people in the organization that ID&E is important. That's the power of dropping a pebble!

Sean's ability to create a shift in stuck thinking took passion, resolve, actions infused with ID&E knowledge, and courage. What we love about this story is that it shows how a wave of systemic change can result from the dropping of a pebble—in this case, turning on the proverbial light bulb in a leader's mind that there is another way to do what has always been done.

We know our approach works, because we've had more wins like Sean's than we can count. Our clients and colleagues come up to us, text us, or send us internal messages proudly explaining how they dropped a pebble, created a ripple that rocked the boat, and had an impact. Folks we've coached report back to us how others have begun dropping the same pebbles, creating their own waves of change. Once they saw what could easily be done to create a more inclusive workplace, they were eager to jump on board and amplify the effort.

We discussed wisdom in the previous chapter, and next we will discuss the notion of having heart on your Inclusive Leadership journey. The fact is that neither wisdom nor heart matter much if you don't have the courage to continually challenge the status quo, to inspire others with a resolutely inclusive approach, and to actually do the work to realize what we all want. As Maya Angelou so beautifully put it, "Courage is the most important of all the virtues, because without courage, you can't practice any other virtue consistently."[1]

That said, think a moment now about the leader who possesses all three: the wisdom to know what to do, the heart to want to do the right thing, and the courage to see it through. That is the Inclusive Leadership trifecta!

# Chapter 4

# DAILY HEART

*Empathy, Compassion, and Vulnerability*

## Carletta Ooton on Listening More Than You Speak

Carletta Ooton is currently an operating partner and head of ESG at Apollo Global Management Inc. She was the head of Amazon's Health, Safety, Security, Sustainability and Compliance (HS3C) organization when we met.

**US:** What does Inclusive Leadership mean to you?

**CARLETTA:** It means leading with the intent to be inclusive, realizing that it is hard and it takes work. It is the willingness to go a different path because you know it is right and will ultimately make your organization a better place to work, even if it would be easier not to do anything different. It is listening as much as or more than you speak, watching the dynamics (said and unsaid) in the room, seeking out team members, and asking honest questions to really learn. It is being empathetic.

**US:** What are the most important characteristics of an inclusive leader?

**CARLETTA:** Humility, empathy, being a good listener, a willingness to challenge the status quo, transparency, being a good communicator, and being fearless in tackling issues.

**US:** Which foundation of Inclusive Leadership resonates the most with you?

**CARLETTA:** Heart, because that was a turning point for me as a leader. At a listening tour, I was sitting with a group of African American employees. Our data clearly indicated that African Americans were not having an equitable experience at work. We were calibrating for [ID&E], looking at all of these data and inputs regularly, but at the end of the day we just weren't making enough progress. We needed to go back and figure out what the heck was going on. Why was it taking two or three times longer for an African American to get to the next level as it was for a white team member?

I credit [coauthor] Jonathan with helping us create the culture at HS3C where people felt comfortable talking about these sorts of issues. We made a plan and agreed on the questions we would ask. I was going to open it up, then tell them I was just going to listen and take it all in, and I wasn't going to try and solve for anything.

I remember one junior-level guy saying, "I can't believe I'm sitting in a room talking with you about this; I've never been in a room with you other than the all-hands meeting for the entire organization."

Well, if that didn't humble me in that minute, then shame on me. I shouldn't be leading big teams.

By the end of the session, I had dug holes in my hands with my fingernails. It's emotional just recalling this memory. It is still to this day so hard to tell you how much it hurt to hear what people's real lived experiences were in the organization I was ultimately responsible for and actually proud of. And it was the best thing that could ever, ever happen to me.

We got to the end. We stopped. It got really quiet. I thanked the team from the bottom of my heart. Outside of an employee telling me about a family member who died, this was the only time that I ever cried at work. I did what I would call blubber balling. I tried to assure them that this wasn't the organization I wanted it to be and that it wasn't good. I was committed to making it better. We were going to look for ways to get together and talk about it. I told them I would share exactly what they said, without their names, with my leadership team.

I've told this story multiple times, trying to articulate the importance of listening to feelings and experiences on top of quantitative data. You can't do just one; you can't do the other. You need to do both and do it well. But if you are not listening to people, and you aren't listening to the right people in the organization, and to the people that don't look like you, the people that are most likely the marginalized people in your organization, or the people who don't feel included, you are screwing up.

Several years ago, and shortly after Jonathan took on a new position, his manager began sharing some personal information with him. They let him know they were going through a very difficult time with an unwell family member. The manager mentioned they would need to leave work, suddenly at times. It was surprising and a bit awkward to hear such intimate information from a manager, but Jonathan didn't dwell on that aspect. Jonathan let them know how sorry he was that they were going through this tough time. He empathized with them about how incredibly difficult it must be and asked how he could best support them. What could he do to help?

A few months later, a member of Jonathan's family became ill, requiring him to take time off each week. When approaching the same manager, Jonathan had no doubt that he could share this information about a personal issue and that it would be well received. He knew that his manager would be empathetic and that he'd get the grace needed.

The manager had dropped a pebble that showed their heart, which allowed each person working for them to show heart. They created a safe environment for each person on the team to be themselves. This inclusive leader took what was a horribly challenging personal experience and used it to swing the work culture to become safer for everyone, more transparent, more vulnerable, and more empathetic. Their leadership style led to stronger relationships, relationships that Jonathan has maintained to this very day.

## THE HEART OF AN INCLUSIVE LEADER

Having heart as a leader means shedding the hard, unfeeling shell you might wear to protect yourself. It means showing up as you are, sharing who you are with others, and creating the space for others to also show up as their whole selves.

Your willingness to share something personal communicates your humanity. Through this exchange, you create a human connection. Your employees will begin to trust that they can also be their vulnerable selves with you.

The reality is that no one can operate at 100 percent every day. We all have lives outside of work that can affect our ability to be our best selves. Babies and parents get sick and need our care; family members pass away; couples get in fights; stress builds up. Inclusive leaders accept that people's productivity will fluctuate and that they need to give their team members empathy and the time and space to heal, to feel better, to adapt.

If you can share when you're not at your best, you allow your team members to feel safe doing the same. Being vulnerable with your team members subtly communicates, "It's okay to be vulnerable with me, and you can expect empathy and compassion in return."

Empathy is an admirable trait, yet we urge you to go a step further, to compassion. Expressing compassion means that you take action to help your employees, to improve their circumstances. This can range from giving them encouragement to temporarily taking work off their plate, lightening their load with budget or people to help, or solving the problem altogether. Showing you care about your people through self-care, encouragement, living your values, and standing up for your principles is having heart.

## CREATING A SPEAK-UP CULTURE

Because you don't know what people are going through at any given time, your team members need to be able to tell you. You need your employees to feel safe coming to you, to communicate how they're doing and what they need from you to best support them. An inclusive leader creates space for people to feel safe to speak up. To speak up when they receive frightening medical news, lose a family pet, or have a family issue that is affecting their performance. To also be free to speak up when they screw up. To speak up when they're in over their heads and feeling they're going to fail. To speak up when they experience bias, microaggressions, insults, and discrimination.

Inclusive leaders support a "speak-up" culture because everyone in the team should feel empowered to say something when bad behavior occurs. It is not enough for you to be passively against discrimination. You must actively speak out against microinequities, stereotypes, forms of ethnocentrism, and unconscious biases, and hold offenders accountable. If you don't stop the behavior in the moment, it becomes normalized, destroying the trust and confidence of marginalized team members. Over time, a culture of exclusion develops, dividing people by in-group and out-group. The culture becomes one of "I belong here, and you do not." When you leave any form of discrimination unchecked, you can quickly affect employee engagement and retention. It can all spiral south fast.

Inclusive leaders have daily practices and processes in place to facilitate these conversations in the moment, before things get out of hand. Two of our favorites are what we call the pause button and calling in or calling out (see chapter 8).

## FOCUSING IN ON THE WHOLE PERSON

Being an inclusive leader requires the wisdom to see the whole person—to see each person as unique and to resist the single story based on a stereotype or bias. It means having the heart to be authentic and true to your values as their leader, while also having the courage to do what is right in any given situation, and not what is expected or easy. Self-reflection and taking time to gain a balanced, fair view of situations are traits of heart and wisdom. This also means making tough decisions with humanity. Be transparent and honest when providing feedback. *Call a duck, a duck.* This is a phrase we like to use as a metaphor for being authentic and real with people. Say what you mean and mean what you say. As an inclusive leader, make the difficult business decisions, yet make them with empathy.

Showing your heart as a leader while encouraging the heart of your team members can have incredible effects on employee motivation, loyalty, and commitment. Doing so has also been shown to reduce stress and increase productivity. If you see something being done well, say something! Create a culture of catching your people doing things right, and share the good news. This leadership behavior will bolster their confidence and contribute to building a culture of belonging. And when an employee's performance falls off, focus on the whole person to begin the conversation.

Ask your employees how their day is going. Then ask again: How's your day *really* going? Tell them you really want to know, then lean in. Listen actively. Crank up your emotional intelligence during these conversations to be aware of how you are coming across. While drawing on your awareness of cultural differences, watch their eyes, body language, inflection, tone, everything. If you sense discomfort, back off. Your employee may not be comfortable sharing at the level you want, and that's okay. This is a great opportunity to practice the Platinum Rule and treat your people as they want to be treated. They will value your awareness and ability to adapt in the situation. Know that you're sending the right message by showing that you care and are there for them, whether that be to listen or to help in the way they need. And that's good enough sometimes.

Paraphrase back what you heard. Ask clarifying questions. Slow everything down to understand their perspective. You may never understand exactly what they're going through, but you can use your ears and eyes to grasp as much as possible. If they stop talking, wait eight to ten seconds, then ask, "What else?" Silence is very powerful. Many people feel the need to fill the quiet, although the amount of quiet will vary by culture. Allow people the time and the space to reflect and share with you. Don't jump in right away with your advice.

Think of a doctor of osteopathic medicine (DO), who takes a holistic view of the patient. When someone is ill, they don't immediately prescribe medication to address the symptoms. The DO looks at the person holistically, including their environment, to understand what could be affecting them, looking for the systemic root cause of any issue. As an inclusive leader, you need to ask yourself, What's going on in my people's lives that could be affecting their work? You need to work to see each of your employees fully. Your people give so much of themselves every day, *and* they have lives outside of work with their own sets of challenges, issues, and accomplishments.

When issues are spiking outside of work, they affect work. Support your people during their hard times and they will give back to you many times over with loyalty and commitment. You'll retain your talent longer. Plus, as a bonus, employees will drop their own pebbles of heart, empathy, and compassion, creating positive waves around you and drawing more talent to your team.

---

It's been said in different ways by different people: we do not lead companies and organizations; we lead people. If you want to be an inclusive leader, you must learn how to lead people. Your people are the key to your success. If you make your employees successful, you will be successful.

But let's acknowledge that demonstrating heart does not come naturally for everyone. We're all different; we come from unique cultures and backgrounds, and we have varying levels of comfort with being vulnerable and open. Also, transparency can open you up to criticism, and you're going to make mistakes. It's all part of the learning and growth as an inclusive leader. We've seen many people promoted to become people managers because of their technical knowledge and skills. These folks are not promoted because they know how to lead people; they have to learn that skill. Leading inclusively is a learned skill that takes practice and study. It is a matter of trial and error over many years.

Get in the ring. Dive into the seven insights so you have the wisdom to lead inclusively. Practice empathy, compassion, and being vulnerable so you can lead with your heart. Have the courage to stay the course on this journey to building a culture of belonging and to rock the boat when you need to.

In his book *The 21 Irrefutable Laws of Leadership*, John C. Maxwell wrote that if you practice leadership, you become a stronger leader. If you don't practice it, you become a weaker leader.[1] It's that simple. The good news? Descriptions of the daily practices of inclusive leaders are coming in part 2.

But first, there's one final critical piece we need to discuss: setting up your organization for ID&E success.

The approach we advocate in this book is most likely to flourish when there are structural and accountability components in place. For larger companies, these may constitute a full-on ID&E infrastructure. For small to medium-sized organizations where there is no distinct ID&E function, it is still critical to understand the scope of foundational elements that can support inclusive leaders' work in this area.

We'll lay out a high-level look at structure and accountability in this last foundation chapter, with an eye to how you can support ID&E in your organization from the ground up.

Chapter 5

# STRUCTURE AND ACCOUNTABILITY

## Laura Clise on Spend Like It Matters

Laura Clise is the CEO and founder of Intentionalist Inc., a Seattle-based online guide to intentional spending that supports small businesses and diverse local communities. She is a Main Street small business champion, LGBTQIA+ activist, and advocate for social change through sports.

As a college student in the late 1990s, Laura heard Judy Shepard speak about her son, Matthew, whose brutal murder was the highest-profile hate crime against LGBT people at the time. Laura recalls Judy's challenge to the audience, to the effect, "If you want to live in a world where people are out at work, you come out so you live in that world."

Several years later, Laura was concerned about the survival of small Main Street businesses and the fraying of the social fabric of our communities. Heeding Judy's words, she reflected, *If I want to live in a world where companies are more compassionate and intentional, then I get there by building companies that are more compassionate and intentional.* So that's what Laura set out to do with Intentionalist.

Laura also knew from her experience at multinational, multilateral organizations such as General Mills, DHL, and Intel, how companies struggle with walking the talk in their commitment to equity and social responsibility. So she and her team set out to help big organizations live up to their commitments with "Spend Like It Matters" (her company's tagline). Intentionalist connects them with small Main Street businesses owned by women, people of color, veterans, LGBTQ-identifying people, families, people with disabilities, and every intersectionality. The model works so effectively that her "tiny" social enterprise company now has the most successful organizations reaching out to her.

*I've learned to ask a lot of questions, and through those questions and listening, I observed a gap and had an idea on how to fill it. That's how Intentionalist was born. I realized Inclusive Leadership is not about any one of us having the answer. We navigate to better solutions to the extent that we effectively tap into, and invite, the awesomeness of others.*

*What Inclusive Leadership yields, and why folks we've partnered with have reached out to us, is the trust of the stakeholders, those organizations who give a damn about Main Street small business, those small businesses that contribute to our cities and communities, beyond the products they have for sale.*

If you're looking for examples of Inclusive Leadership, they're in the small local businesses, Laura says. Small business owners recognize that there are much easier ways to make money. They know that their value is in more than selling the products and services available for purchase. Their value is in how they center community, people, and connection in an authentic way.

*They are living, breathing examples of what is possible when we put people first, when we put community first.*

*When we recognize that value is created through connection and relationships, and when we provide an inclusive space to build belonging.*

Intentionalist hopes to seed a culture of Inclusive Leadership in the larger organizations they partner with that reflects the Inclusive Leadership seen in the small business community.

By the way, Intentionalist also makes it easy for everyday citizens to find local restaurants, bars, gyms, shops, and more owned by historically underestimated, marginalized, or oppressed people. According to Laura, it all starts with everyday decisions about where you buy a cup of coffee, work out, or pick up a birthday gift. So drop a pebble and buy from a small Main Street business today!

Structure and accountability enable sustainability, authenticity, and norms to be baked into the culture of an organization. These efforts are what create the inclusive environment we know is critical for the success of any ID&E strategy. Without structure and accountability, ID&E efforts lack a strategic anchor and are, at best, well-intentioned, one-off activities as opposed to a series of pebbles that create a ripple effect of systemic change.

Please note: the structure and accountability efforts in this chapter are largely bigger asks than the daily practices of inclusion we explore in part 2. However, once they're in place, they lead to a slew of ripple-causing daily pebbles that leaders can buy into across organizations and teams. Think of structure and accountability as means of investing in dedicated diversity resources; creating a robust ID&E strategy with global goals and targets; establishing business mechanisms for reviewing, discussing, and holding teams accountable for goals and targets; establishing a means of communicating efforts both internally and externally; and building out the infrastructure to do all this with intentionality. The pebbles that we will discuss in part 2 are ones that you can drop, and combine with and flow from these larger efforts, leading to sustainable systemic and cultural change.

We understand, however, that not every person reading this book will have the power, nor will every organization have the resources or infrastructure, to implement all the recommendations in this chapter. Not every company, for example, can invest in dedicated ID&E professionals to drive this work. We realize that smaller companies will have to be scrappy and find ways to do this work internally or contract it out on a smaller scale. Hiring ID&E consultants is a wonderful workaround to help create and implement ID&E strategies, trainings, and processes.

For leaders at smaller companies, our recommendation is to take in this structure and accountability discussion with an eye to implementing the pieces that make sense for your firm. There will undoubtedly be nuggets you can pull that will amplify the ripples that come from dropping daily pebbles of inclusion. Consider what you have the capacity to take on in-house and what you may be able to outsource. And later on, in chapter 9, we focus on an important scaling mechanism that is hugely beneficial for companies of all sizes, but particularly those with small or nonexistent ID&E teams: using human resources (HR) professionals as true ID&E partners.

## HIRE A DEDICATED ID&E LEADER

Hiring a dedicated ID&E leader—or allocating dedicated time and ID&E ownership to an existing leader—signals seriousness to the organization's employees, to its customers, to its competitors, and to the marketplace. Our advice: if you want to hire someone to lead ID&E, first negotiate headcount, budget, and executive sponsorship, because once you are aboard the boat and out at sea, it's challenging to reach your destination without the right equipment. Depending on the size and hierarchy norms of your organization, the leader could be a vice president, director, or program manager. The level matters because it indicates how important ID&E is to the business; however, just having a point person for ID&E efforts is a great first step.

Whom the leader reports to also matters. For the role to have the respect of and access to senior leaders across the organization, it must be positioned alongside other critical business functions. If the role is buried in the org chart, it's like being in the engine room of a ship with little to no access to the captain's bridge. As a strategic business issue affecting every corner of the organization with direct impact on the bottom line, ID&E should report to the top, ideally to the CEO. The most common reporting line is ID&E reporting into HR, but we do not recommend this organizational structure. A key role of HR is to manage the legal risks that stem from employees' actions. Now, consider that a critical priority for ID&E is to advocate for employees who are having a different, more negative, and possibly discriminatory experience. The possibility of conflict between these two mandates is obvious, which is why we believe the two functions should be separate. We have enjoyed many fabulous HR business partners through the years, and many HR leaders are wonderful advocates and allies. You will read in chapter 9 just how valuable a partner HR can be to ID&E. However, we believe it's best to have ID&E report up through the business leadership directly.

Another reporting line we've seen is ID&E as part of talent acquisition. This gives the false impression that ID&E is all about recruiting and hiring people of color, women, veterans, and people with disabilities. But ID&E needs to be embedded in every stage of the life cycle, which is why we don't recommend this reporting structure either.

# BUILD AN ID&E STRATEGY AND INTEGRATION PLAN

There is no one-size-fits-all ID&E strategy and integration plan. Every organization should have its own strategy to address its very specific identified needs. What works for one may or may not work for another, which is why ongoing assessing, monitoring, and adjusting are critical to the success of any ID&E program.

At a high level, the five phases of building an ID&E strategy and integration plan are as follows:

1. **Preparation:** start the conversation and get buy-in.
2. **Assessment and review:** understand where the organization is today and where you aspire to be in the future.
3. **Planning and development:** create a gap plan from the identified issues, challenges, and opportunities identified in step 2.
4. **Implementation and monitoring:** determine who needs to get what done and by when, as well as how you will track progress.
5. **Version next:** assess the status of your initiatives on a regular basis; listen and learn; adjust and pivot to ensure that your actions are having the desired impact.

In the chapters that follow, you'll read about the specific daily practices we recommend as a part of your plan. But here's one we want to emphasize for every phase: prioritize transparency and communication. Doing so will go a long way to support the credibility of the work. Drop pebbles through consistent and effective communication of what is being done, why, and where you are in the process. In emails to the CEO, president, and department leader, in newsletters, on posters, and on your intranet website, let people know what's happening and how they can get involved. Big ripples can result from encouraging participation across the company.

## COLLECT ALL THE DIVERSITY DATA AND DISAGGREGATE IT

Diversity data is a powerful tool for identifying gaps in recruiting, hiring, workforce representation, and terminations between the majority population and historically underestimated and marginalized people. In fact, we recommend that one of the first hires after the ID&E leader be a senior ID&E data analyst. If that's not possible, consider building a relationship with your organization's data analytics team to leverage their skill set.

Failing to collect and track diversity data is a structural barrier to understanding what needs to be fixed. Be sure to collect and analyze all the demographic data you can legally request of your employees in your country or region. Capture the layered details that will allow you to uncover masked trends. This is where data intersectionality and disaggregation come in. Intersectionality in this context refers to collecting data in as many categories as you legally can to better identify trends. Disaggregation is the process of purposefully breaking down data into its many component parts. For example, instead of looking at race data rolled up into broad categories like white and underrepresented minority (URM), you disaggregate the data (if legally allowed to) into white, Black, Asian, Latine, Indigenous, and so on, so you have more specific information pointing to where the actual issues exist.

Let's say you want to answer the question, Do we have a gender issue with women hitting a ceiling in their pursuit of senior levels? Data that isn't disaggregated might indicate that there's a gender issue that you need to solve. With disaggregated data, however, you might discover that the problem isn't simply a gender issue but an issue only for Black, Latina, and Indigenous women, as they have a 4× gap relative to white and Asian women's growth in the organization.

Shortcuts and sticking your proverbial wet index finger in the air to see whether you are moving in the right direction do not cut it. Making intersectionality and disaggregation a mandatory aspect of all demographic data creation, assessment, and reporting enables you to intentionally target limited resources and eliminate a wasteful scatter-shot approach to solving negative trends. Common ID&E categories of data in the US are race, gender, age, veteran status, and disability. (Sexual orientation and gender identity information is something ID&E professionals and other leaders talk a lot about but have not consistently captured.) Globally, data collection varies depending on country or region. In many countries, it is common to collect gender data but not the intersection of gender and race, with South Africa being a notable exception. On a global level, it is also important to collect data on ethnic or cultural identification, especially given the amount of immigration there is between countries. Work with your legal team to make sure you are doing this right.

We also recommend collecting data on structural categories, such as tenure, geography, and level. That way, you can begin to see how people who belong to multiple underserved or marginalized groups are demographically stratified in your organization. We guarantee it will be illuminating!

ID&E leaders should set the expectation that all data sets will be functionally capable of disaggregation and intersected with as many demographics and business-related variables as make sense. Doing so will signal your expectation that everyone in your organization needs to act and lead inclusively every day. This will also be noticed and appreciated by underestimated and marginalized employees who often feel they are invisible and not appreciated as part of what makes their organization great.

From our experience, leveraging diversity data takes courage and a willingness to rock boats. Having such illuminating data on hand can make legal teams and representatives extremely nervous, especially if comprehensive guardrails and guidelines for use aren't spelled out. We've participated in more significant strategic disagreements about diversity data than about any other aspect of ID&E work. But the benefits of having the data we needed, and having it accessible to the people who needed it, were well worth it. One of the smartest moves we made in building our ID&E team at Amazon was to hire a dedicated data analyst, Allie Sydnam. Eddie often says that she was the best hire he ever made. As we said, however, if you don't have the luxury to employ a dedicated data analyst, see how you can partner with the leader of your organization's HR people analytics team to get what you need.

The ripples that will roll through your organization from demanding this level of data sophistication will be profound. Your people-related life-cycle decisions, which you make daily, will be more on point and purposeful. You will be able to close the most pressing demographic gaps you have, making your strategic efforts as fruitful as possible. You will save time and limited resources because of this laser-focused approach. More important, this precision will lead to increasingly equitable and fair outcomes for all employees throughout every aspect of the life cycle everywhere in your organization.

# IMPLEMENT TARGETED HIRING REFERRAL PROGRAMS

Employee referral programs are valued by organizations because hard-working, talented people tend to know other talented, hard-working people. Studies back up these assumptions: referral hires have been found to be more engaged at work, less likely to quit, and more productive.[1] And for employees, the cash offered can be motivating.

Employee referral programs can work well for hiring a diversity of talent as well. When social media company Pinterest instituted a targeted employee referral program, it enjoyed a 24 percent increase in women referred and a 55× increase in the percentage of referred candidates from underrepresented backgrounds. At multinational consulting firm Accenture, its targeted referral program goes beyond ethnic and racial backgrounds to include people of different religions and faiths and education levels, as well as single parents, first-generation immigrants, and college students. Bonuses can range from $2,000 to $7,000, sometimes even more.[2] At Intel, a referral for a "woman, minority, or [military] veteran" who gets hired earns twice the standard referral bonus of $2,000. In a talent pool that is disproportionally made up of white males, the company views the bonus fee to boost the representation of women and minorities as well worth it.

As for all referral programs, you will need to collect and track data to understand what's working and what's not. In addition, make sure your leadership team speaks out regularly about the program's importance and value at organizational meetings, in one-to-one meetings, and meetings with people leaders. But perhaps the most important tip for ensuring the success of a targeted referral program to increase diverse representation is to implement a multipayout system. For example: 20 percent of the bonus (or whatever incentive is motivating) is given for candidates who earn a formal interview, 60 percent for candidates who get hired, and the remaining 20 percent after the first-year anniversary of the referred employee. Remember: the goal is not just to get a diversity of hires in the door; it is to make them want to stay. This system of incentives encourages the referrer to stay connected with their referral and participate in building a culture of belonging.

## RECRUIT FOR DIVERSITY

It's been our experience that talent acquisition (TA) strategies far too often result in replicating the status quo. They operate under the false assumption that diverse talent is too difficult to find or is absent altogether. Unfortunately, the way many TA professionals are incentivized to do their work does not support intentional recruiting. Their focus is often on bringing in as many candidates as they can in the shortest amount of time. Consequently, to meet their numbers and time constraints, they tap the same sources repeatedly. One way around this is to hire a dedicated diversity recruiter or candidate sourcing specialist and add specific goals and targets for hiring historically underestimated and marginalized people. There are also plenty of high-quality consulting companies and recruiting agencies who specialize in diversity recruiting.

We also recommend that leaders get personally involved with programs such as diversity invitationals and diversathon sourcing events. Diversity invitationals are sponsored recruiting events where potential candidates are brought into a company for a day to meet with executives, recruiters, diversity professionals, and other key individuals. The goal is to create a list of potential candidates from a range of underrepresented backgrounds that can be tapped quickly when opportunities open up. Diversathons are three-to-four-hour focused talent sourcing events where recruiters and business leaders gather and work together to generate an increased diversity of job candidates. Both types of events can put the company on the radar of very talented potential employees.

If a leader is willing to spend their time or advocate for their teams to spend time partnering to find a diversity of talent, then TA professionals are more likely to make this one of the focal points of their daily work. Business leaders like you are the TA professional's internal clients. This is where you can "spend your privilege" (more on this in chapter 8) to start a ripple effect of change.

## PARTNER WITH ORGANIZATIONS THAT SUPPORT UNDERREPRESENTED GROUPS

Diversity recruiting is arguably the most competitive arena in recruiting. Everyone is vying for the same talent, and when you intersect "diversity" with positions where the pool of talent is already narrow—for example, software engineering, artificial intelligence engineering, and customer service[3]—the organizations with a view to the far horizon will win.

We all know that you have to put money in the bank before you can make withdrawals; this also applies to diversity recruiting. To build a sustainable diversity recruiting machine, organizations must make a long-term investment in relationships with professional and technical associations focused on communities of historically underrepresented and marginalized people. Some examples are the Society of Women Engineers, the National Black MBA Association, the American Indian Science and Engineering Society, Lesbians Who Tech & Allies, and the Wounded Warrior Project. For a long list of accredited national organizations, visit the resources section in the back of the book.

We recommend getting actively involved at the national level and, where local chapters exist, locally as well. Many more people tend to be active at the local chapter level, so that's where you can make the most immediate impact. Investment at the national level is valuable, but it's typically a long game to see substantial results. It takes time to build trust and a positive image, brand, and reputation when events are only held annually.

At the local level, you can speed the process of building trusted relationships through more regular interactions, such as by attending monthly or quarterly chapter meetings and social events, sponsoring or providing expert speakers, hosting events at your local office, funding food and drink, and volunteering for chapter leadership roles. Association events can be fabulous opportunities for the majority culture at your organization to *respectfully* grow their cultural competency and to support their personal ID&E work and learning journey.

If you have members of a certain community in your organization, specifically ask them to get involved. It's incredibly valuable for people outside your organization (i.e., future job candidates) to see people like themselves in your organization. It is particularly valuable when hiring managers and organizational leadership from underrepresented communities get involved. The more visible they are, the better. To the extent that your employees are comfortable participating in local chapter and national events, encourage them to join the diversity recruiting team as "ambassadors" or honorary members of the recruiting team, similar to employees who are members of an organization's diversity leadership team.

Senior leaders and recruiters should attend annual national conventions as well as participate as members of the recruiting team. Our experience is that conference-goers want to speak to the business leader if possible and not just the recruiters. It may be a big ask, but your presence will send ripples in every direction, so get there if you can. Word of this type of commitment within diverse communities at a company adds to the authenticity of ID&E efforts.

Important note: when working with historically underestimated and marginalized people, trust is a huge factor. How can the potential job candidate know how inclusive your work environment really is? How can they know they will not be an "only" or a "token hire"? The idea of making deposits to the bank account before making withdrawals is all about trust. You build trust and earn credibility by investing the time to listen, learn, and connect before sharing job opportunities. For more detailed advice on how to listen, learn, connect, and share, see the "Show Up for ID&E" daily practice in chapter 7. And when members of professional and technical organizations begin to approach *you* about your organization's open roles, you will know that your deposits are paying dividends.

## INTEGRATE ID&E INTO ONBOARDING AND MANAGER ORIENTATION

You don't get a second chance to make a good first impression, so including ID&E in the onboarding process can have a tremendous impact on employee engagement and commitment, affecting motivation and reducing turnover during year one. ID&E communication at this crucial moment should come from the organization's leaders (CEO, VPs, people leaders) and include information about opportunities to get involved and support the diversity of the workforce. It's a powerful pebble to drop because you're connecting with employees when they are new, a time when people are most open to change.

Invite your ID&E leader or another ID&E professional to present at onboarding sessions. They should provide information on the organization's values, the commitment to ID&E (possibly in the form of an "equity statement"), employee resource groups (ERGs), community outreach and engagement, recruiting, learning and development opportunities, current diversity data, and organizational ID&E goals and targets.

Whenever possible, invite leaders of your ERGs to attend onboarding events and present information on their groups' structure, programs, activities, and events. Invite employees to sign up as members of that community or as allies (allyship is discussed in chapter 7)— everyone should be welcome to get involved. Sharing community outreach and related engagement initiatives with employees can also show folks that the organization takes seriously its responsibility to the communities in which their employees live, work, and play.

If you have a targeted employee referral program, or even a generic employee referral program, you'll want to leverage your new hires as a resource for more good people, so promote that referral program at onboarding. Friends and family of new employees will be asking about their first day. It's a great opportunity to create ripples in the community to recruit additional talented people.

Be sure to talk up your ID&E training programs and encourage new employees to utilize those early months to take available courses: Inclusive Leadership training for people leaders, inclusive hiring training for those involved in the hiring process, and for everyone else, basic ID&E training to establish a shared understanding across the organization. Then quickly follow with courses such as How to Be an Ally and Cultural Competency that give people very specific daily practices that they can start immediately. Show them the pebbles to drop that will create the ripples of change. Making these practical courses a priority is one way to spread the work of building a culture of belonging throughout the organization.

Share diversity data and be transparent about gaps, "cliffs" (levels at which the percentage of people from underrepresented groups begins to sharply decline and the majority population sharply increases), issues, and challenges the organization is experiencing. This is a quick means of establishing trust and credibility. When you communicate candidly about the challenges being faced, you earn employees' trust. The more quickly you can earn that trust, the more committed and motivated employees will be to deliver their best work.

Last, inform everyone about the organization's ID&E goals and targets and share progress over time. Provide new hires with the context to grasp the organization's ID&E journey from where you were, to today, and where you aspire to be in the future. When new employees return from their orientation session, they'll inevitably be asked about their experience. When they share with colleagues that ID&E is an organizational priority, they're dropping pebbles that communicate ID&E's importance.

## DEVELOP DIVERSITY-FOCUSED MENTORING AND SPONSORSHIP PROGRAMS

Mentoring and sponsorship of historically underestimated and marginalized people are two impactful methods of supporting employee retention, increasing diversity at higher levels of the organization, and building a more equitable culture.

Such programs provide employees from underrepresented groups with knowledge and resources that may be inaccessible to them through informal means, such as how to navigate the organizational culture and its unwritten rules of success. It can be especially inspiring for mentees from historically underestimated and marginalized groups to learn from mentors with similar lived experiences who have already achieved success within the organization.

In **one-to-one mentoring**, specific senior-level mentors are matched with lower-level mentees based on common interests, career paths, and even identities. **Mentoring rings** provide scalable group mentoring for employees across an organization, including both peer-to-peer and senior mentorship. Cohorts of women, people of color, and others coming together with similar interests and experience can reap the same benefits of ERGs, including community and peer support, along with the added value of senior-level guidance.

But perhaps the most important approach in terms of dropping pebbles of inclusion is reverse mentoring. This is where the mentor becomes the mentee! The value comes from a lower-level mentor, typically from an underrepresented group, helping to grow the senior-level mentee's awareness, understanding, and knowledge in any number of topics, particularly those related to the inequities the mentor faces.

There is still a higher percentage of leaders who are white, male, able-bodied, cisgender, straight, and taller and thinner in size—to name just a few dimensions of diversity that bring additional power and privilege to the individual. It is not uncommon for such leaders to have less awareness, knowledge, and appreciation of the lived experience of people who come from entirely different backgrounds and experiences; they may even lack sensitivity. Getting real: if you're a leader who at times is insensitive to or ignorant of the challenges and difficulties of people who hold less power and less status, drop a pebble right here by recruiting a reverse mentor. Start the wave of change in yourself and in a host of other leaders by encouraging them to also participate.

A reverse mentorship is usually between a senior person of the dominant, majority culture and a lower-level individual from a minority culture. Remember, we use the "dominant, majority culture" phrase because in different geographies around the world, the demographic of the dominant group varies. In most western cultures, the reverse mentor will be a person of color of any gender and the reverse mentee a white person of any gender or other intersectionality. In

Japan, the mentee may be Japanese while the mentor is from Korea or even an immigrant who is Latine or white. What makes the relationship valuable is that the reverse mentor has license to hold a mirror up to the leader and reflect to them exactly how their behaviors are impacting people in the organization who are different from them.

Mentees in reverse mentoring relationships are dropping a pebble simply by being vulnerable enough to participate in this radical learning experiment. They are creating the space for the mentor to share their lived experience without the risk of retaliation. They are using their organizational power to understand when and how exclusion and discrimination show up and, more important, to do something about it.

An important note here: we encourage leaders to be exquisitely sensitive to the dynamics between people of higher and lower levels of power working together. If you're a reverse mentee or part of the dominant demographic in the organization, make sure the relationship centers the reverse mentor and their needs. It is a lot to ask of someone lower in the power structure to be vulnerable about the issues they are experiencing with someone who can alter the course of their professional career. Make it as easy as you can for them. Reassure them that this is a safe space.

Also, do not center your philanthropic volunteerism. In white dominant cultures, this is referred to as playing the "white savior." The term was coined by Nigerian American writer Teju Cole and is "the belief that white people are here to save, help, teach, and protect their non-white counterparts."[4] Rather, practice the Platinum Rule. The focus should not be on you, your growth, or how you can "save" others. Rather, it should be on cultivating a positive experience for the other person.

It's an immensely powerful example when a leader openly shares their need for growth and development. Their doing so makes it feel okay for other leaders in privileged positions to do the same. Growing the awareness, empathy, and compassion of leaders at the top who can create change for the overlooked people lower down the ladder is exactly what is needed to build a more inclusive culture.

Whereas a mentor provides coaching, advice, resources, and contacts, a **sponsor** is much more involved in the success of the sponsored. They do all the work of a mentor, plus they collaborate directly with the employee's manager to steer the direction of the employee's career. Sponsors put their credibility and professional reputation on the line by advocating for the employee in public and private settings. For the employee who comes from a community that has been historically overlooked, the sponsor provides valuable visibility throughout the organization.

The sponsor meets directly with the employee's manager as their quasi-agent to learn about the employee from their manager's perspective. What does the manager believe the employee's strengths are? Areas for improvement? What gaps exist for the employee that might delay promotion to the next job level? How does the manager judge the employee? A savvy sponsor can even learn what biases, stereotypes, and ethnocentric beliefs the manager may hold that would inhibit the employee's success. A culturally competent sponsor can use their unique position to educate a naive manager on the challenging path of an employee who experiences microinequities, microinsults, prejudice, and discrimination daily. In this instance, the sponsor's coaching can be as valuable to the manager as it is to the employee being sponsored. Sponsorships drop two pebbles for the investment of one! The growth in the employee's manager has the potential to positively impact all the other employees working for that manager now and in the future. In that way, sponsorships become "superpebbles" with ripples of impact touching many more people in their sphere of influence.

# WEAVE ID&E CONTENT INTO TRAINING

ID&E must be woven into the fabric of the organization. Every decision an organization grapples with should be viewed through an ID&E lens. "How will this impact the business?" becomes "How will this impact our employees, our shareholders, our customers, all their dimensions of diversity, and our culture of belonging?"

Operationally, it makes sense then to weave ID&E content into each learning and development program offered in the organization, from privacy and cybersecurity training to code of conduct and sexual harassment training.

All training courses should involve an ID&E professional or hired consultant from inception to planning and design, then throughout development, testing, sign-off, and delivery to ensure that ID&E values and considerations are baked into the solution. For example, it's important to avoid words, phrases, imagery, or graphics that may be politically, culturally, or geographically offensive. ID&E and cross-cultural expertise throughout the process can help avoid costly rework due to any unintentional oversights. Leveraging your ERGs as well as employees in the market where the training will be offered is another way to ensure that the needs of employees from various groups are being met.

Making ID&E a pillar of all training ensures that everyone in the organization has greater awareness of the blinders that cause them to make culturally insensitive, inappropriate, or discriminatory mistakes. The upside is that when every single training is rolled out to the workforce with ID&E naturally baked in, everyone begins to see and expect it. The effects extend infinitely from the initial splash. Leaders will be more aware of the considerations they need to make for different groups to help those employees feel seen, heard, and valued.

# OFFER OPPORTUNITIES
# WITH THE ID&E TEAM

ID&E teams are often underresourced. Not having enough people or budget to accomplish all of the work required has been an ongoing challenge during our careers. However, being resource constrained has inspired our creativity and innovation. When you don't have adequate headcount or budget, you still have to figure out how to accomplish necessary tasks. Here's our creative way of tapping into more resources, with the added benefit of getting more people across the organization invested in ID&E success.

We've worked with many fine people who believe in the work we do and have graciously given of their time, experience, and knowledge to support the ID&E work. Employee "volunteerism" not only assists in implementing ID&E programs but also helps scale them up. "Volunteerism" is in quotation marks because we believe this work should not be piled onto the employee's existing workload. ID&E contributions should be valued on the same level as core work responsibilities. All "volunteers" should each have a percentage of their time allocated to related projects—5 to 10 percent is usually sufficient to make an impact. In addition, they should have related performance goals and be rewarded for their ID&E work at review time.

Employees who volunteer to work on ID&E projects expand the impact of ID&E without adding headcount to the ID&E team. In addition, their volunteerism builds a broad and deep foundational structure for ID&E in the culture. One way we've organized volunteers is through the creation of a diversity leadership team (DLT), sometimes referred to as a diversity steering committee or diversity champs network. The DLT is led and managed by a full-time ID&E professional; the volunteers each have a percentage of their time allocated to DLT projects. Another option is an ID&E rotation program that allows employees to spend six months to a year working full-time on the ID&E team. The long-term payback is that the employee gains greater awareness and Inclusive Leadership experience to apply to their core work once the rotation is over. Consistent application of both the DLT model and the rotation program can have a massive impact on building a culture of belonging as they create an ever-expanding number of ID&E champions across the enterprise.

Another creative method we've used is to ask the most senior leader of a large division to pay for ID&E headcount out of their budget. The hired ID&E professional would report directly to our ID&E team; we would manage that individual, and they would support that senior leader's division. This created a "center of excellence" model whereby the ID&E subject-matter expertise was centralized in our team. For the senior leader, their large division enjoyed all the benefits without the management overhead requirements.

## EXPAND THE SCOPE OF EMPLOYEE RESOURCE GROUPS

Employee resource groups (ERGs) help build community for groups that have historically been underestimated, marginalized, or oppressed, or that have experienced discrimination in the workplace. ERGs should also be leveraged as strategic contributors to the success of ID&E initiatives.

Everyone benefits from well-resourced and valued ERGs. When important decisions are being contemplated, ERG members can inject incredibly valuable feedback to interrupt bias, stereotypes, and ethnocentric thinking, and identify opportunities the business might otherwise miss. And, as consultants to the business, ERG members know that their stories and perspectives matter, that they are in a place where they belong.

The organization can benefit from the knowledge and experience of ERG members in all areas of the business. For example, working closely with product planning, product development, sales and marketing, and customer service, ERGs can help to ensure that the organization prioritizes "localization" not only by country and region but by customer segment. This was never a one-size-fits-all world, and organizations that have a diverse workforce that mirrors their diverse customer base—and whose voices are heard—are set up for success.

One of the teams Jonathan led at Microsoft was to review products, services, and all marketing materials to ensure that they were politically, culturally, and geographically appropriate in markets around the globe. Any error put Microsoft at risk for negative sales, brand, image, and reputation impacts. Our US-centric thinking had to be kept in check to avoid issues coming back to bite us. At both Microsoft and Amazon, product groups and marketing were encouraged to leverage the vast number of ERGs for cultural insights on how products, services, and initiatives might be viewed by people from non-US cultures.

ERGs have also opened up new markets for businesses. Amazon's Black Employee Network, led by Rovina Valashiay and Kimberly Hill, had the idea around 2018 to launch a new line of hair-care products for Black women and men.[5] Working with Jeff Wilke, the consumer president at the time, they were able to create the storefront on Amazon.com called "Textures and Hues."

## MAKE COMMUNITY OUTREACH A PART OF YOUR STRATEGY

The human tendency is to spend time with people like ourselves. Programs that foster regular, ongoing engagement with a diversity of people in the community can widen employees' exposure to and appreciation of differences. This is how they learn to see people as individuals and not as group stereotypes. This is how they develop the wisdom, heart, and courage to practice inclusion daily inside the office and out.

We have strongly advocated for leaders to add a community outreach component to their team offsites. Eddie made this a practice at Amazon by replacing one of our "team dinners" with a volunteer opportunity at a community-based organization—for example, a food bank. The work sent ripples of purpose and hope through the team, giving everyone a meaningful sense that giving back is important. From the community's perspective, we provided a needed service and sent a message that our company and our team had a community-focused mission that was authentic.

Community outreach efforts can also support your ERGs by intentionally spending time in the communities that reflect who they are. Examples include speaking at local schools, inviting organizations to visit the offices, and volunteering in nonprofit organizations or on city boards and commissions with an ID&E tie-in. For example, Jonathan serves on the board of trustees for Youth Eastside Services, a nonprofit organization focused on the behavioral health and substance issues of youth and their families in Bellevue, Washington. He also has served on the City of Kirkland's Human Services Commission supporting at-risk people for the past six years.

Drop a pebble of encouragement by recognizing employees for their ID&E community outreach work. Facilitate this growth by coaching employees on how to respectfully engage with different communities. As we will discuss in chapter 7, the priorities when engaging with a diversity of people should be to listen, learn, connect, and share—in that order. Like allyship, community outreach is an act of humility. You're not a superhero swooping down to save the downtrodden—you're a helper.

# TARGET YOUR SPEND TOWARD LOCAL MINORITY-OWNED BUSINESSES

There isn't a day that goes by when leaders aren't requisitioning something, ordering food for an event, buying team-branded merch, contracting with vendors, or taking a highly sought-after potential executive to lunch. The normal rhythm of the business involves spending budgeted dollars that support our strategies. This is a great opportunity to drop daily pebbles across an organization that impact a diversity of businesses. Think of this not as giving undue advantage to certain businesses but as creating access for organizations that have historically been denied equitable opportunities.

The pebble could be targeting a percentage of spend toward local businesses owned and run by Black and Brown people, women, people with disabilities, military veterans, LGBTQ-identifying people, and so on. Our advice is to increase that annual spend, year over year, until your strategic targets are met. The daily practice of spending precious resources equitably will manifest across your entire organization, with resounding impacts. This is literally spending your privilege!

By advocating mindful diversity-focused budgetary spending, you are signaling to minority businesses everywhere your company is located that they matter and that you will be contributing to their success. This really is a win-win situation. Selfishly speaking, the more you spend with minority-owned businesses and the more wealth you create within these communities, the more likely they will become your loyal customers.

Here's a great add-on pebble: increase the impact of your targeted spending by communicating these efforts broadly and often. Communicate that your company truly understands the systemic issues that many minority-owned businesses face and that you want to be allies, accomplices, and community partners.

This will hit close to home for so many of your employees, and it's free advertising for the businesses! It will also create opportunities for employees to engage with these minority vendors—to listen, to learn, to connect, and to share. The knowledge and learnings from these conversations will guide you even further on your ID&E journey and support you in building a larger community of belonging that includes employees and the local community.

## OFFER UNWAVERING SUPPORT

We've experienced what it feels like to be supported 100 percent and also, unfortunately, what lip service feels like. This work is hard and can feel massively unappreciated, disrespected, and overlooked, so when we know someone has our backs, it makes all the difference. When leaders offer unwavering support, guidance, and shared accountability, it serves as an ID&E journey accelerator for the organization and for building cultures of belonging.

Here's a funny but telling illustration. Eddie hung a sign in his office that had a bull's-eye on it with the words, "Hit your head here." He made it clear that if anyone on his ID&E team ever felt as though they were hitting a (metaphorical) wall, all they needed to do was knock, point at the sign, walk in, and hit the literal wall. That happened more frequently than you would imagine, and it led to so many empathetic and productive discussions: What's up? What can I do? How can I have your back?

A daily practice for leading inclusively can be as simple as overtly and visibly supporting ID&E leaders in whatever way they need to be successful. Support can be actively backing the ID&E leader in a meeting, inviting them to senior leadership meetings and offsites, creating visibility for them with the board of directors, and highlighting them and their efforts in communication vehicles. It can be providing dedicated time to meet with anyone driving ID&E efforts. It can be including them in as many rhythm-of-the-business activities as possible (e.g., weekly team meetings, leadership reviews, marketing discussions, monthly or quarterly talent reviews, employee engagement or attrition discussions, and any other process structure that creates the foundation of the organization's commitment to ID&E).

If you want to foster organizational and cultural change and build a culture of belonging, proudly and visibly have someone's back. Have the courage and heart to stand side by side with any one person, team, or committee chartered with ID&E strategic imperatives. Use your privilege, position, and power to ensure that efforts are taken seriously and are given the same respect as any other business imperative, and to show that you are 100 percent behind the effort. This support can't merely be words; it needs to be action, resources, and participation. Having a "got your back" mentality requires having skin in the game and fostering an allyship culture.

This daily practice will send a ripple throughout the organization which communicates that others should support ID&E work in similar ways and signals to specific communities that the organization understands the importance of ID&E and is invested in it. Hiring a dedicated leader, building and implementing an ID&E strategy, and collecting the right data are significant foundational efforts, but any daily practice that illustrates buy-in and support, and inspires others to do the same, will contribute to organizational and cultural change.

# Part 2

## THE DAILY

## PRACTICES OF

## INCLUSIVE LEADERS

W ork, engagement, success, and impact are all embedded in
systems. These systems are not linear; metaphorically, they're
like a sphere with interconnected threads throughout. When you pull
on one thread in one part of the system, there is a reaction or impact
in other parts of the system.

The following four chapters illuminate the life cycle of an employee
and highlight a sampling of daily practices and pebbles you can drop at
each stage: attracting talent; developing, keeping (retaining), and engaging talent; and leading inclusively every day. Visualize these chapters as an interrelated and operationalized sphere. As inclusive leaders,
we all must challenge ourselves to understand the connections among

the foundation we build, the talent we attract, and the working environment we create.

Understanding what it means to lead inclusively at each stage of the employee life cycle will open your eyes to just how many opportunities there are to drop pebbles of inclusion and encourage those around you to do the same. As we've described earlier in this book, some daily practices manifest as pebbles you drop once that lead to a slew of other pebbles being dropped and ripples of change washing over an organization. Other daily practices can literally be done every day; all they require is a mindset shift, heightened awareness, and vulnerability. We designed these daily practices so that they do not add significantly to what you already have on your plate. It would be a major barrier to leaders' ID&E journeys if this were the case! The beauty of these daily practices is that they are not "extra"; rather, they fit seamlessly into the rhythm of your workday.

# Chapter 6

# ATTRACT

Talent acquisition is an initial entry point for many organizations who are starting ID&E efforts. While attracting a diversity of talent is clearly important, we believe it is a mistake to center an entire ID&E strategy around it. Remember: attracting talent is just one of the many important 3D pieces in the employee life cycle.

What happens when you focus primarily on attracting diversity without training your leaders in how to manage and engage difference and how to build a culture of belonging? Best-case scenario: diverse talent feels underestimated and unseen, and becomes disengaged. They certainly won't be your organization's biggest champions. That kind of organizational branding can seriously impede diversity recruiting efforts! Worst-case: you end up with an attrition sinkhole. If people feel as though they don't belong, they will most likely leave.

Many efforts to broadly attract talent consist of pebbles that you drop once and that lead to a slew of smaller, ripple-causing daily pebbles. These include creating a robust global talent acquisition strategy, setting very specific diversity-focused global goals and targets, and creating the links to key stakeholders across the organization.

## PRACTICE CANDIDATE SLATING

At many companies, there are noticeable cliffs. Candidate slating is designed to reduce the drop-off at these points or to increase representation when there are identifiable gaps in a job group. Slating is the practice of ensuring that two or more people from underrepresented groups are interviewed for any open position. The idea is to create access to opportunities where there might not have been access before. Once folks have access, they can compete for the roles like everyone else.

Candidate slating is often used to increase the number of people from underrepresented groups at senior levels. The downstream and long-term impact of having more diversity at senior levels is an overall increase in representation across teams and the organization at large. At Amazon, we experienced firsthand how the numbers of women and people of color grew faster when there was a woman or person of color at the helm. The leader becomes a bellwether to attract talent that looks like them. Employee retention goes up, too, because people see people like themselves in leadership roles and believe that's a realistic path for them. Slating has a "flywheel effect" to attract, retain, and grow representation over time.

Research reported in the *Harvard Business Review* indicates that having at least two people from underrepresented groups on interview slates significantly increases the likelihood that these job candidates will be selected for the role. However, the chances are reduced to nearly zero when only one person from an underrepresented group is on the slate.[1]

# ASSEMBLE INTERVIEW PANELS
# WITH DIVERSITY IN MIND

A diverse panel of interviewers can lead to a significant improvement in the percentage of historically underestimated and marginalized people hired. According to a survey by hiring software company Greenhouse, "68 percent of candidates believe that a diverse interview panel is fundamental to better hiring experiences and outcomes, showing that [ID&E] is top of mind."[2] For technology conglomerate Cisco, creating a diverse interview panel framework helped them increase the number of women interviewed globally by 14 percent. The company's research also showed that the new framework would likely improve the chances of hiring Black candidates by 70 percent, and Hispanic and Latino and women candidates by 50 percent.[3]

Intel requires there to be at minimum two women or people from historically marginalized groups as interviewers. As a result, it has seen a dramatic increase in the diversity of hired job candidates. According to Danielle Brown, Intel's VP of HR, "Implementing diverse hiring panels has enabled us to cast a wider net at the outset of the hiring process and systematically help reduce unconscious bias in our hiring."[4]

Like Cisco and Intel, we recommend collecting data to track your organization's success. How many hiring managers are dropping the pebble of implementing diverse interview panels? What has been the impact on representation over time?

# HIRE FOR SOFT AND HARD SKILLS

Although the culture at our former employer Microsoft has evolved over the years, it took an intentional and herculean effort to build a culture of belonging because, historically, managers were hired for their specialized technical capabilities without an adequate assessment of their people (i.e., soft) skills. Soft skills had to be taught, developed over time, and then evaluated during performance reviews.

Managers who can't demonstrate empathy and compassion, or lack the confidence and self-security to be open and vulnerable, can build a grueling, dehumanizing culture in which morale suffers, turnover is high, and work/life harmony is nonexistent. For folks outside the majority population, the experience can be even more harsh. Many will struggle to work under these ill-equipped managers who lack the skills necessary to lead inclusively. This is why it's so important not to overindex on hard skills when recruiting talent—doing so can be a huge hindrance to building a culture of belonging. Soft and hard skills are equally important to be successful.

We've seen some encouraging developments in this space over the years. At Amazon, teams create "tenets" that act as guiding principles about what is important to their team and, by default, about what is not. In Eddie's consulting work after he left Amazon, he presented a couple of times to an engineering group in Amazon Web Services (AWS). As a result, the VP leader of this very technical team added empathy to their list of tenets. Jonathan had a similar experience with his client Transpo Group, a transportation engineering firm based in Kirkland, Washington, which added empathy to its company values. This pebble had the ripple effect of emphasizing the importance of this "soft skill" in creating the inclusive team chemistry they wanted.

# Chapter 7

# DEVELOP, KEEP, ENGAGE

Treat your employees like volunteers. The reality is that your employees aren't required to work for you. They can leave at any time. And it's been shown that the number-one reason employees leave an organization is their manager. It makes sense then that managers should treat their employees in a way similar to how they'd treat a volunteer. It's a leadership mantra we developed after serving on several volunteer boards and commissions.

So how do you treat a volunteer? Consistently demonstrate your commitment to them through your behavior. Support their professional and personal goals. Advocate for them and their work. Mentor and coach them to be more successful in their efforts. Recognize and reward good work. Always be recruiting: never stop giving them reasons to stay and contribute at a high level.

In this chapter, we'll provide you with daily practices that zero in on how to demonstrate your appreciation and commitment to people, particularly those who have been historically underestimated, marginalized, or oppressed. We'll reveal ways to create very positive and fulfilling experiences by creating community, through mentoring and advocacy, through executive-sponsored programming, through organizational resources, and by weaving ID&E into the daily rhythm of the business. In aggregate, these daily practices will evolve the culture to be more inclusive, increasing everyone's motivation and commitment to perform at their highest possible level, to grow their knowledge and stretch their skills, to be positive role models, and to believe they can enjoy a long and mostly happy and satisfying career with the organization.

## WHO'S IN YOUR KITCHEN?

During our Inclusive Leadership training sessions, we pose the question, "Who's in your kitchen?" When you entertain at home, who are the folks congregating in your kitchen (as they always seem to do)? These are the people you spend the most time with, who get to know you at a deeper level, and whom you get to know equally well. If your friends are limited to the folks who look like you, think like you, and have a background and culture similar to yours, then you're limiting your world to a narrow few. It becomes very difficult to grow your cultural competency and your comfort with people different from yourself if you're only spending time with people similar to you.

The question originates from Martin Luther King Jr.'s time in Alabama during the US civil rights movement. The social justice leader and his collaborators enjoyed plentiful meals in the home of Georgia Gilmore as they planned their strategy and tactics. Dr. King posed the question while thinking about the time his team spent together in Gilmore's kitchen.[1] If only more of us spent time with people different from ourselves in one another's kitchens, how much greater understanding and empathy would we have in this world?

So, who's in your kitchen? If the diversity of people is lacking in your personal life, you'll find it tough to be comfortable with folks outside that demographic at work. Connecting with a diversity of individuals at work will also be difficult if you always spend your social time at work—for example, lunch, coffee or tea breaks—with the same people every day.

On a daily basis, take steps to expand the circle of people you spend time with. Ask someone new to lunch, grab coffee or tea with somebody from a different culture than your own, utilize ID&E events and really all your social opportunities to connect with a diversity of individuals. Use the time to get to know them, learn about their work, and how they experience the work environment. What is their lived experience? What are their interests and hobbies? Their views and perspectives? Listen with the intent to understand and to build bridges. Follow the listen, learn, connect, and share approach detailed in the next section.

Over time, this practice will increase your skills as an inclusive leader. Your new knowledge will factor in when reviewing resumes, interviewing job candidates, considering the makeup of your team, and determining what needs to be changed. In the process, you'll be changed, and the people around you will be equally and positively affected. Pebble. Ripple. Wave of change.

## SHOW UP FOR ID&E

Have you ever heard the phrase, "Eighty percent of success is showing up"? Your physical presence at ID&E events sends a strong message that inclusion, diversity, and equity are important to you personally and to the organization.

Participating in ID&E-related events will enhance your credibility as a leader and help you build connection and trust with your historically underestimated and marginalized employees. Be vocal about your plan to attend, as this will encourage others. Share your plans with team members and your network of leaders. Invite a colleague in another department to join you. Two pebbles dropped cause a bigger ripple than one!

We're all living superbusy lives, and events outside our control can affect schedules. Set a personal goal to show up for ID&E events and set the expectation with your team to be there. Yet keep in mind that less than 100 percent attendance isn't failing. If you miss an event, stay dedicated to your commitment and be there for the next opportunity.

Showing up is valued, and it's equally important to know your role and your purpose at ID&E events. Your role as a leader in the organization is to listen, learn, connect, and share.

**Listen.** Hear what other people have to say—their stories, views, ideas, thoughts, and opinions. Let them know that they matter. Ask precise questions to go deeper in your conversations. Paraphrase back what you hear, or ask clarifying questions to confirm understanding. This is how you build a culture of belonging: question by question, conversation by conversation, pebble by pebble.

**Learn.** Open your mind to different ways of seeing the world. Make note of anything that challenges your own way of thinking so that you can explore the topic further. Write down the names of people you meet, recommended books, ID&E influencers mentioned, YouTube videos and podcasts to watch, and social media accounts to follow. These are the pebbles other people are dropping for you, so be sure to catch them.

**Connect.** Expand your circle to expand your perspective. Invite people who are different from you into your kitchen. If you find it challenging to introduce yourself to new people, take it one pebble at a time. At the first event, maybe you connect with just one new person.

That's great! Just keep on going. Remember, sustainable change comes from the aggregation of small, consistent actions. With every new person you connect with, you are gaining new insight into the daily practice of leading inclusively.

**Share.** Use these events to be of value to others. Drop the pebble of sharing information and resources that can give people from historically marginalized groups a hand up. Your network and the information you hold from years of experience as a leader in the organization can be a treasure to others. Being a resource for underserved groups has the cascading effect of making people feel seen, encouraging them to reach new heights, and gradually leveling the playing field of access and opportunity.

## ENSURE PROMOTION EQUITY

A great way to undermine a culture of belonging is to overlook high-performing employees from historically marginalized groups while people who represent the dominant culture rise up the ladder. The reason members of the dominant culture get promoted at a faster clip can be argued as complex, yet it's really quite simple: people promote people like themselves. The demographically dominant group will naturally spend more time with people like themselves. They'll receive additional information, support, time, development opportunities, visibility. It will be easier to promote these folks because they are in an inner circle that is being set up for success. For the same reason, employees who have been historically underestimated, marginalized, or oppressed are seen as less likely to succeed at higher levels and get judged more harshly at performance review time.

It's simply harder to get promoted when you are not part of the dominant demographic of an organization. We saw this in our work when it took three to four times as long for Black and Latina women to get promoted, even though they had the same or higher performance evaluation scores. This is incredibly deflating to the people treated inequitably, and leads to a vicious cycle. The overlooked employees withdraw, and their lack of participation leads to impaired perfor- mance, which makes them less likely to be seen as promotion mate- rial. And once these folks are perceived as underperforming, they are left to languish without support.

Drawing direct attention to promotion inequity with data is a powerful pebble you can drop to turn the tide. Review promotion data with an intersectional lens so that you're looking not only at men ver- sus women but also, for example, Black women's promotion rates versus those of white women, and white men versus Latine men. Analyze for patterns within departments and with specific managers to under- stand where the managers could be responsible for the impacts of bias on the employee experience. Create awareness among leadership and people managers, then hold managers accountable for these patterns when discovered. Build strategies and tactics to anticipate and prevent these forms of discrimination from happening in the first place with specific ID&E training that addresses talent management. Include ID&E professionals in the talent review discussions while priming those discussions with information to interrupt bias and stereotypes during the actual talent review process.

Creating opportunities for interactions with senior leaders is an- other important yet simple daily practice that results in more equita- ble talent management decisions. We can't tell you how many times we've been in promotion discussions or employee rating meetings and heard a key decision-maker say something like, "I really don't know much about Malcolm, but I've been consistently impressed with Al- isha and her performance, especially her presentation last week; we should consider promoting her."

The simple practice of creating visibility for a person of color, a woman, a person with disabilities, or someone who is a cultural minority takes almost no effort, but can be a game changer. As a leader, you may have the everyday privilege of, for example, getting in front of your organization's executive team. You are the one behind the podium speaking to the entire organization at the quarterly all-hands meeting. You are the one tapped for another critical task group to solve an external branding issue. Use these moments to create visibility for someone from an overlooked group instead! Give them the opportunity to present, to sit on the task group, to be a part of the high-potential program, to feature their work in a client meeting. The trust you show to people who feel unseen and the visibility you create for them can pay huge dividends in building a culture of belonging—and for very little spent privilege.

In our experience, using data to hold managers accountable for promotion inequities, coupled with creating visibility for people from underrepresented backgrounds, completely changes the dynamic in talent management meetings. These practices impact promotion rates and employee ratings significantly. But there is another subtle but powerful ripple that dropping these pebbles causes. As more high-performing employees from overlooked groups rise through the ranks and excel, more space opens up for real dialogues on the value of ID&E to the business. In our work, these discussions enabled us to tie our ID&E efforts to the business, to positive customer impacts, and to creativity and innovation. We learned that one of the best ways to foster organizational and cultural change is to make ID&E a legitimate topic of conversation at all the key inflection points in the rhythm of the business.

## BE AN ALLY AND AN ACCOMPLICE

Consider who gets interrupted in a meeting, who gets chastised for taking a controversial or contrarian position, whose ideas and achievements get appropriated, and whose opinions are categorically questioned or discounted. Consider the Black man who is told in a meeting to "settle down" when exhibiting enthusiasm during a robust discussion. Think of the person with autism who's chastised for not making eye contact or for their difficulty reading social cues. Or the hiring manager who always uses male pronouns in conversation, assuming the candidate hired is going to be a man. These are but a few examples of opportunities for allyship or being an accomplice.

An ally is someone who supports individuals and groups of people who are victims of inequities. More recently, the term *accomplice* has arisen to describe someone who risks their own standing to speak up when inequities occur. Showing up as either is a noble and selfless act. Doing so is about supporting others who, in many instances, have had a different lived experience than you have and may lack the power and privilege that you've experienced.

There is, however, a larger role for people born with the most inherent privilege and power. If you are a straight, white, able-bodied, neurotypical cis male born into wealth, for example, it's important to acknowledge the privilege those aspects convey to you in most societies. You can choose to use that privilege for your own benefit, or you can spend it on lifting up those who were not born with the same societal advantages. Those of us born with the most privilege have the greatest responsibility to drop pebbles that rock the boat.

In the words of Toni Morrison, "If you are free, you need to free somebody else. If you have some power, then your job is to empower somebody else. This is not just a grab-bag candy game."[2]

You cannot call yourself an ally or an accomplice, but when you commit to the daily practices we've listed here, the person or group you are supporting may view you as one.

1. Examine your own biases.
2. Learn about the histories of oppressed groups.
3. Get comfortable talking about uncomfortable topics.
4. Accept feedback with humility.
5. Keep your antennae up to recognize bad behavior.
6. Speak up.
7. Don't make it about you.

Being an ally is of significant value in the moment to the people you are supporting, but the long-term value comes from modeling allyship behavior for everyone around you to see, time and time again. Pebble by pebble, you are showing what it means to be inclusive and making it okay for others to be inclusive as well. Further, you are making inequitable behavior less acceptable because offenders know that it will not go unnoticed. These are the ripples that lead to building a culture where everyone feels safe to stand up for victims of inequities.

## MAKE PRIMING YOUR FRIEND

Think of priming as a simple daily practice to mitigate the unconscious biases influencing your decisions during talent, promotion, and resume reviews, or other evaluative processes. As we discussed in chapter 2, all humans have biases, conscious and unconscious. We favor what reminds us of us. Because of this reality, our decisions about potentially life-altering job evaluations, promotions, and hiring can be far from objective or equitable. Priming doesn't eliminate our biases, but it very effectively interrupts unconscious behaviors by making us more conscious and present during the task at hand.

Priming involves creating a list of very key characteristics, skills, or attributes most relevant and salient for whatever people-related process you are engaged with. For example, you could write a list that includes five crucial leadership characteristics, three most important company values, and two key skills required for a particular promotion opportunity. You read your priming sheet after each candidate review to ensure that you're evaluating the candidate using the most important criteria. Getting locked into a repetitive process can put us in the automatic, unconscious zone. Taking breaks to review the priming sheet also facilitates your staying conscious and focused.

The ripples of priming can be astonishing for both the organization and the individual. For an organization, the daily practice of priming can be one of the key drivers of increased percentages of a diversity of hires and thus overall representation. It can make promotion decisions significantly more equitable. Priming helps individuals become more aware of their personal biases, which makes them better equipped to drop more pebbles of inclusion and to model for others what it means to be inclusive. The result is significant waves of awareness, equity, and critical inclusive norms.

## HOLD INCLUSIVE ONE-TO-ONES

A valuable tool available to leaders in building a culture of belonging is the one-to-one meeting. It is a widely underrated mechanism for building connection with direct reports.

For individuals who come into the workplace with less power, less status, and less privilege in society, the one-to-one meeting is a distinct opportunity for their managers to build psychological safety and a sense of belonging, to communicate worth, to demonstrate support, to encourage, to protect, and to motivate and inspire them. The pebbles leaders drop in one-to-one meetings can also spur employees to create stronger connections with their direct reports (if they are a people manager) as well as their colleagues. Here are our tips for holding inclusive one-to-ones. Some may seem obvious, but in our experience, most leaders could use the nudge to make these practices habitual.

1. **Make the one-to-one a recurring event on the calendar.** Leaders spend time on activities that will propel their business success. A recurring calendar event communicates that the employee is important to the success of your business. When scheduling conflicts arise, ask to reschedule instead of canceling.

2. **Be on time.** This shows respect for the employee's time while sending the message that they matter. They are worth your time, and you want to hear what they have to say.

3. **Change the conversation and setting occasionally.** Get out of the office and meet over coffee or lunch or, if you're both physically able, take a walk together. Changing things up to be less formal may help both of you relax and be more comfortable sharing information. Leaders create connection when they show an interest in their direct reports' personal life and goals outside of work.

4. **Let them set the agenda.** You may have a couple of items to share, but remember, this is their meeting, and their agenda should be paramount. Try to avoid status updates that can be accomplished through other means and encourage the employee to arrive with a prepared agenda, ideally sent to you beforehand.

5. **Celebrate wins!** Not everyone enjoys public recognition, so the one-to-one is an ideal time to let the employee know that you value and admire their achievements. And for those who enjoy public praise, there's no crime in doubling up and thanking them both privately and publicly.

6. **Demonstrate vulnerability to build trust.** Ask for feedback on your performance: How am I performing for you as your manager? Are you getting what you need? If there's one thing I could change about my behavior or leadership, what would that be? Don't defend your behavior or justify any action; just listen and seek to understand. Feedback is a gift, so when the employee shares, be sure to thank them. The Platinum Rule applies!

7. **Focus on your employee's strengths.** Acknowledging their unique talents and abilities can be especially impactful when you're doling out a new assignment. Let them know you see the gifts they bring to work every day and why you believe they can execute this new task well.

8. **Ask precise questions.** This communicates to your employee that you are engaged and listening. Take notes on your action items or follow-up commitments; it's a great way to let them know that what they are saying is valuable.

9. **Inform your employee of changes that will impact them directly.** The most respectful way to communicate changes is one-to-one. If there are plans being discussed, gain their perspective. This is effective in letting people know that their opinion matters, and an excellent opportunity to implement point 8.

10. **Ask how you can help.** Where does your employee need you to be involved? This may include attending a meeting,

sending an email, giving them more independence, connecting them with someone in your professional network, or escalating an issue when needed. Show that you are there to be of service. Demonstrate that you have their back!

Keep in mind the need to style-switch when working within a multicultural environment. It's safe to say that some of our recommendations may prove challenging in some cultures, particularly numbers 4 and 10. For example, it may be harder for folks who grew up in a culture with a more rigid hierarchy to speak openly and candidly to individuals more senior than themselves. In these cases, you may need to observe their nonverbal cues to get at what they are really thinking. It may take more time and more direct encouragement for them to feel comfortable sharing. Your own vulnerability and willingness to share are pebbles that will ease the communication door open.

## SET ID&E PERFORMANCE GOALS

In 2016, Microsoft created accountability for ID&E goals by tying performance on ID&E to executive compensation. Three years later, the company updated its performance review process to incorporate inclusion goals for every employee, "referred to internally as a DEI Core Priority, a set of actions based on personal reflections that are meant to align with and promote the company's DEI priorities for that year."[3] We highly recommend tying ID&E performance to employee evaluations to increase accountability. A study by the Society for Human Resource Management highlighted that fifty-one companies on the S&P 500 had a diversity metric in their compensation program in 2018. Three years later, "that number had nearly doubled to 99 companies."[4]

SMARTIE goals are an evolution of SMART (specific, measurable, achievable, relevant, time-bound) goals. They include ID&E accountability by ensuring that your goals are **inclusive** and **equitable** and are effective mechanisms for weaving ID&E into the daily rhythm of the business. Although your organization may not mandate that every people leader or every employee have an ID&E goal, you can drop a pebble by requiring all the employees on your team to carry a SMARTIE performance goal. Here are some examples to consider:

- Evaluate compensation of 100 percent of team members for equity and correct any inequities by end of Q2 (July) 2024.
- Ensure that 100 percent of interview panels include at least one woman and one person of color by end of fiscal year (December) 2024.
- Increase supplier diversity spend in my business unit by 20 percent over prior fiscal year.

The impact of adding *I* and *E* (inclusion and equity) to the more common SMART goal format hits when employees slow down and assess whether the outcome of their work is truly inclusive and equitable. This is how you rock boats.

ID&E goal setting drops the pebble that this work is important and valued by the organization. A second pebble is the tracking and communication of measurable progress. With data in hand, you can facilitate more discussions on ID&E and openly celebrate accomplishments. A third pebble you can drop is to share employees' ID&E performance goals with their colleagues and managers. Create ripples by encouraging them to adopt the same strategy for their teams and offering to coach them through the process.

# ID&E EFFORTS AS PROMOTION CRITERIA

We recommend including ID&E responsibilities in job descriptions so that the expectation is set, up front, that contributing to ID&E is part of the job. Taking it a step further, consider adding ID&E goals to job promotion criteria. This single pebble can have a real multiplier effect. When you build daily practices into the systems of the organization, you create a sustainable process that will create waves of change long after the process is initially implemented.

By embedding ID&E into the very fabric of advancement, the organization is sending a clear and strong message that ID&E is highly valued, is foundational to the organization's success, and improves the work environment. It also communicates to every employee that they are an integral component of the efforts to advance inclusion, diversity, and equity.

We recommend building a list of substantive ID&E activities that are valued by the organization; this list will help employees understand the type of work they can do to document their impact. Each time an employee is up for promotion, they must document their efforts to further ID&E within the organization. A list of sample ID&E activities are available to view from the Resources section in the book. If you and/or a leader identify a gap, then you should create an action plan to close that gap.

# CELEBRATE WINS, SUCCESSES, AND LEARNINGS

If we were handing out pearls of wisdom, one would be, don't ever allow your ID&E effort to feel like a black box. ID&E wins should be shared, celebrated, learned from, and used to model an inclusive style of work. Clearly and frequently communicating about your efforts—for example, an ID&E outreach program success, a business leader integrating ID&E successfully into their engagement strategy, or even a missed target to close the gap in the number of women in senior management roles—absolutely serves to authenticate efforts.

The goal of celebrating wins is to create visibility and buy-in for the organization's ID&E efforts. Any communication should encourage involvement and give hope to those who feel as though they don't belong. Transparency in ID&E work is also a powerful way to garner creative ideas, involvement, debate, and accountability. Openly communicating about what you are planning, what you are doing, and what the end results are should be a pebble you drop daily.

A CEO ID&E awards program is one of our favorite methods of communicating wins because of the engagement it sparks and what it conveys about the importance of ID&E work. Here's what an award program could look like: Employees are nominated for this award based on ID&E work they were engaged in, internally or externally, that had an impact on one or more of the points of the employee life cycle. The selected winners, say three per quarter from different geographical locations, are invited on a call to share their stories with the CEO. We have fond memories of the CEO of one of our previous companies surprising the winners and other nominees in Japan by walking in on their celebration so that they could celebrate together in person. Robust communications, screen shots, verbatims, and pictures put in a newsletter or company-wide email had the ripple effect of increased participation, dialogue, and the belief that ID&E was an important strategic imperative for the company.

Employees clamoring for visibility leveraged this program to implement passionate ideas, and their work proved, without a doubt, that diversity and global diverse perspectives fuel creativity and innovation. It was almost impossible not to be influenced by the waves of ID&E energy. Employees also saw themselves in the multitude of programs and efforts they read about or participated in. This experience fostered a clear appreciation for the company's buy-in and contributed to building a culture of belonging.

Other initiatives to promote ID&E internally include newsletters, reporting on ID&E at all-hands meetings, and sending out a weekly "inclusion tip" in team emails. But this is far from an exhaustive list. The bottom line is to come up with simple, strategic practices that fit your organization's norms to communicate ID&E wins, successes, and learnings on a regular basis.

# Chapter 8

# EVERYDAY INCLUSION

Have you ever wondered how an organizational culture is shaped? Take a minute to consider the acceptable and unacceptable behaviors, interactions, and aspects of your organization's culture. Have you ever thought about how you would change that culture for the better?

How would you inject questions or processes that would motivate people to stop, even for a second, and consider how their words and body language are impacting those around them? When an inappropriate joke is told by a member of the opposite sex, what do you do? What would you say to inspire your coworkers to increase their self-awareness and modify their communications? Can you reduce the number of microinequities that people in your organization face? Can you help people feel more connected to one another?

We believe you can.

In this chapter, we share with you our proven daily practices for creating positive and meaningful dialogue with others. These practices help you to pause and think about how your words and nonverbal communication affect others. They help you become more effective and inclusive communicators and leaders. And they are as valuable in your personal life as they are at work.

## LEVERAGE MICRO-OPPORTUNITIES FOR INCLUSION

There is greeting by the Zulu people of South Africa that occurs in two parts: the first is *Sikhona*, which means "I am here to be seen"; the second is *Sawubona*, which means "I see you."[1] This awareness of humanity, of seeing another person who works alongside you, transcends cultures.

When walking around the office, you as a leader are not invisible. You will be seen, and your behavior, conscious or unconscious, will increase or decrease your stock as an inclusive leader.

Whom you say hello to and whom you choose to pass without a nod can make an (unintentional) statement about who you believe matters. This is why chance encounters are fabulous micro-opportunities to examine your biases and practice inclusion. Be aware that people see you, and show them that you see them too. Smile or nod. Say hello. Make eye contact if you are able and it is culturally appropriate—while being aware of the differences in nonverbal language between neurotypical and neurodivergent people. These actions may seem simple enough, but we guarantee that making them a daily practice will have a huge impact on your employees. They might even energize some people and put a little extra skip in their step.

You know that all people want to be seen, heard, valued, and understood. But it's especially important to acknowledge employees who regularly feel unseen—or worse yet, are subject to microinequities—because of some aspect of their identity. A daily practice of saying hello is a small pebble that quickly creates ripples around the office. It sets the expectation that everyone, regardless of race, gender, job level, and so on, is worthy of acknowledgment. It is one small yet powerful step in building a culture of belonging.

## FIND YOUR VOICE

Inclusive leaders always have their antennae up for inequities—in meetings, the lunchroom, and office hallways. Interactions of all types should have folks feeling supported, that they are a part of the team, and positively connected to one another. When they are not, however, the active management of behavior—live, in the moment—is where you can drop the most impactful pebble. Whether you're leading the meeting or simply participating, you have a responsibility as a team player, as a person with a vested interest in the success of the meeting, of the team, and of the organization to help correct wrongs or injustices when you see them.

All employees should be vested in building a culture of belonging; no one needs a license to use their voice. If you're in a building and you smell smoke, whose job is it to say something about it? Everybody's. Similarly, if you see a behavior or hear about a decision that you believe works against the company's culture of belonging, you have a responsibility to use your voice. You have a responsibility to jump into the conversation, to ask the questions to spur a different way of thinking, and to motivate personal reflection.

Finding your voice means saying something about the ignorant whispers as a Muslim woman walks by, about the coworkers who discount the comments an "only" makes in a meeting, about the person who continually and intentionally misgenders a transgender teammate. It's easy to stay quiet and watch people get cut down when you're not directly impacted. But when it happens to you, you'll be grateful that someone had the awareness and the courage to speak up for you. Be that person for others. Lead from the front. Find your voice.

Not everyone will find their voice in the same manner. Depending on a multitude of factors, speaking up in the moment can be harder for some than for others. Finding your voice may be as subtle as clearing your throat, tilting your head, or raising your eyebrows at the opportune moment. The goal here is to do something to disrupt the bad behavior—how you do that is up to you. We all need to use our voices because the ripples from doing so will have profound impacts on engagement, learning, awareness, and feelings of belonging.

When people observe you speaking up to support a teammate, you're modeling positive behavior for others to emulate. When they see you doing the right thing, they learn. They learn ways to do what is right and that it is okay to do it. They begin to practice speaking up and supporting others.

## HIT THE PAUSE BUTTON

When you hear or see something that might be upsetting to another person, it's best to hit the pause button and discuss the issue in the moment. The pause button gives everyone permission to stop the conversation, to prevent moving on to the next agenda item or topic when more conversation or introspection is needed. When a team member says, "Hold on, let's hit the pause button" or "Wait a minute, I'm hitting the pause button," this is a cue to everyone in the room that they need to slow down and think more critically and with greater contemplation before moving forward. Here are some examples from our own lives.

- At a talent review meeting with divisional leadership when we were presented with a list of the lowest-rated employees, and eight out of the ten were Latine or Black (true story)

- When evaluating job candidates for a software development engineering role and we realized every single one of them was a man
- When discussing a potential hire and one of the interviewers expressed concern that the candidate wouldn't be a good fit for the culture

These are all situations in which it would be appropriate to hit the pause button. Challenge everyone to talk through why certain groups of people are being left out or targeted. Check to see whether bias, stereotyping, or ethnocentric thinking are playing a part in the outcome.

The pause button is an agreed-on technique you introduce to the team and organization, then practice repeatedly until it becomes part of your work culture. It is a pebble you can drop during any kind of interaction, formal or informal. It takes the pressure off the seemingly constant desire to go, go, go, when the best choice would be to stop, pause, and reflect. Hitting the pause button is very effective when dealing with topics that are emotional, uncomfortable, and difficult to discuss, especially in an environment that doesn't foster a "speak up" culture.

When you hit the pause button, the next step is to ask questions that challenge the way everyone involved sees what just happened. Here are a few examples to get you started:

- What are we not seeing?
- What conversation are we not having?
- What would happen if we changed our perspective?
- Imagine someone else making this decision; what would they see?
- What arguments could we make in opposition of our decision?

- What are the assumptions underlying the decision that we believe to be true?
- How are personal experiences, beliefs, or cultural and societal norms shaping our perspective?
- Did we allow enough time to gather and consider all data, as opposed to making the quickest or easiest decision?

The pause button can interrupt biased thinking and impact decisions throughout every phase of the employee life cycle. Practice using it daily. Then watch it catch on as it becomes a part of your organization's culture.

## ASSUME POSITIVE INTENT (MAYBE)

Inclusive leaders try to give someone the benefit of the doubt when what the person said was racist, antisemitic, ableist, sexist, or exclusionary in any way. You let them off the hook at first because you assume that their intent was positive or at a minimum neutral. You assume that cultural differences, generational differences, or language differences, for example, probably explain why they said something inappropriate or acted in a way that was demeaning. This doesn't mean you let it slide; it just means you don't immediately call them out or label them as discriminatory. Assuming positive intent does often work to head off feelings of defensiveness and more quickly enables the situation to move to a moment of learning and awareness. That is all positive.

It is important, however, to address the "maybe" aspect of assuming positive intent. There will be times when you don't assume positive intent, and it is perfectly justifiable not to. Situations when, for example, Black people are constantly and inappropriately asked to speak for all Black people. This is so commonplace, so frustrating and demeaning, and such an immense weight on their shoulders that assuming positive intent in the moment is not effective. It needs to be okay for the Black person in that situation to speak up, to call the question or statement out as inappropriate, to explain the implications of asking that question, and to state how it makes them feel. It will be a learning opportunity for anyone willing to listen. But the Black person in this situation also doesn't have to be the one to speak up and deliver the learning moment. Speaking up as an ally or accomplice will go a long way toward building credibility as an inclusive leader and provide evidence to marginalized people that they are not alone in this battle.

We've had people excitedly share with us how they watched situations unfold and learned from it, so that the next time they could speak up about it. When you model both assuming positive intent and pushing back when assuming positive intent is too much to ask, you are contributing to the building of an inclusive workplace.

## DECIDE WHETHER TO CALL IN OR CALL OUT

Related to assuming positive intent is the "calling-in" approach to handling moments of conflict, perceived bad behavior, or disagreements. "Calling in" refers to using calming, nonaggressive language and/or questions to handle a disagreement, or to point out inappropriate comments or behaviors. The main goals are to acknowledge the offense committed and its harmful impact *and* create the space for learning without defensiveness.

In a group setting, calling in occurs the moment you hear or see something wrong. The pebble you can drop and the ripple you can cause when you call someone in, in front of others is powerful. Why? The ensuing dialogue can help the offended party feel safer and supported. It sends the message to them—and to everyone else in the group—that they matter. Calling in can also take place in private when it is important to prevent the offender from losing face, a term that originated from the Chinese concept of *tiu lien,* or suffering public disgrace. Either way, calling in is a respectful conversation that taps into one's compassion for the offender. It requires the courage to listen first, fully understand the other person's perspective, and refrain from lashing out.

Calling out, by contrast, is a much more direct and often emotional approach to shutting down bad behavior. The goal is not to build camaraderie or have a learning moment, necessarily. It is about leaving no doubt that the behavior was not acceptable.

As inclusive leaders, we've all wrestled with when to call in versus call out a transgression. It's not a decision to make lightly. Take this example: Someone in a meeting makes a comment about another person's accent, mocking them in jest. Calling someone in at that moment might sound like "I'm curious. What was your intention when you said that? What is driving your discomfort with their accent?" By contrast, calling someone out might look like "Wow. Nope. Ouch. That is inappropriate at best. I don't find that funny in the least, and you owe them an apology."

One response might solicit learning, and the other might cause defensiveness, but choosing your approach is more complicated than that simple dichotomy implies. While calling in might feel better and keep the situation from escalating, you need to recognize what that very moment might represent for the person who was the target of the microinsult. It's likely not the first time it has happened nor the first time someone has respectfully tried to call in the offender. When the targeted person is already weighed down by constant microinsults, the best thing an ally or accomplice can do for that person may be to shut down the toxic behavior with a clear callout. That needs to be understood and okay. When people are involved, complexity reigns!

You will need to make decisions every day about when to call in or call out. One rocks the boat harder in the moment, but both can have profound long-term impacts on behavior, team chemistry, moments of learning, and even feelings of engagement, psychological safety, and belonging. We don't feel that it is our job to draw the line for you as readers and leaders. It is important, however, to understand the potential impacts of either approach and to have a heightened awareness of why calling out might be more appropriate in a given situation.

## THINK THROUGH INTENT VERSUS IMPACT

When we talk about intent versus impact, we often show the words on a slide with a red equal sign with a line through it ($\neq$) to signify that intent does not equal impact. What someone means to say or do does not always match up with how their words or behaviors actually land. And when the impact is negative, "I didn't mean it that way" does not absolve a person of responsibility. Think of it this way: if you step on someone's foot by accident, the impact is a hurt foot even if there was no intent to harm. It's still important to acknowledge and repair the harm. The same logic applies here.

The clue that intent has not equaled impact is the unexpected reaction of the other person. It may be what they say or don't say, or some nonverbal cue. For inclusive leaders, having the awareness and ability to read someone's facial expression or body language is an extremely valuable skill. You also might not hear about the situation in the moment, but later from that person or from someone who has the courage to approach you and point out the misalignment between intent and impact.

Impact may not equal intent because of cultural differences, generational differences, language differences, lack of awareness, or, unfortunately, a lack of empathy. This is where the foundations of Inclusive Leadership come in, particularly the seven insights from the 2IL model: cultural competence, ethnocentrism, unconscious bias, stereotyping, microadvantages and microinequities, the Platinum Rule, and being a tempered radical. The more you own and understand those seven insights, the more they will help you to reduce intent-versus-impact issues—and to respectfully repair any harm when necessary.

Here's an example: Eddie gives someone very tough, direct feedback intending to motivate the recipient, but it has the exact opposite effect. Understanding the Platinum Rule (treat others how they want to be treated) and our human tendency toward ethnocentrism (believing our cultural way of doing things is the only right way) would go a long way toward helping him understand why he did not have the impact he intended and to take a more effective approach with this employee the next time. The question we ask you to consider in situations like this is, are you willing to really listen, be vulnerable, and, where appropriate, apologize and make it right? That is leading inclusively. That is sending a positive ripple of understanding about you as a leader and what you expect others to do in similar situations.

Think critically about the impact you have in each of your daily interactions. Personalizing your understanding of the seven insights will grow your awareness of when your intent does not match your impact and help you to narrow any gaps. This daily practice strengthens your Inclusive Leadership and models the type of respectful and inclusive behavior that contributes to a culture of belonging.

## PRACTICE INCLUSIVE BRAINSTORMING

The act of brainstorming isn't exclusive to any specific culture, though the name might be. Brainstorming is an open, no-holds-barred group discussion to generate ideas, solve problems, or test what people are thinking about. The goal is to get every idea out on the table, and the premise is that there are no bad ideas. It can be a very effective technique to quickly generate a laundry list of ideas, but it can be problematic for people who are neurodivergent or introverted, or whose primary language is different from the norm, or in situations where certain people dominate the conversation. In other words, when you solely rely on brainstorming, you might *not* be getting the best, most innovative ideas to solve your problems because not everyone is contributing.

The pebble you can drop here is simple: level the playing field for contributing. Prior to your meetings, send out a message to let everyone know the topics you plan to discuss in the meeting and where you are looking for generated ideas. Encourage people to prepare their thoughts beforehand; they can respond to the message or bring their already generated ideas to the meeting. You can also make it clear that ideas are welcome for a certain period after the meeting. The inclusion of options for how and when people can present their ideas enables every person to participate in their own way and ensures that no ideas are left on the table.

The ripples from this simple pebble are huge. For the team members who don't feel heard because of how and when they communicate best, this daily practice of inclusion can significantly up their level of contribution and sense of belonging. If you use clear ID&E business-case language when providing these options for participation, you also indicate to team members that diverse perspectives equate to more creativity and innovation. Ultimately, they will see the benefit, as the wider range of ideas generated will push the business to find new, more effective ways to operate and serve customers. We encourage you to use this practice as a jumping-off point. How can you create a diversity of options for participation in other types of meetings and team activities?

## MAKE MEETINGS INCLUSIVE

Our introduction to inclusive meeting practices came from Patti Falconer, an ID&E leader for many years at Microsoft and Amazon. In the competitive, frenetic world of high-tech companies, behavior can get out of hand quickly. In the pursuit of higher productivity, people can lose sight of respect, dignity, and common courtesy. Patti's goal was to create new meeting habits that changed the meeting culture to be more respectful and inclusive. She created a list of inclusive meeting tips and posted them in Amazon conference rooms throughout her business group.

With the posting of the Inclusive Meeting Tips posters, a pebble had been dropped. People took notice and talked about the tips. Many teams adopted a quick sixty-second routine of starting their meetings with an inclusive meeting tip and a discussion of why it was important to follow. Some tips came from the poster, and others were new ideas that bubbled up from employees. All helped to create awareness, educate, and send a strong message to everyone about the importance of creating and supporting an inclusive environment.

More pebbles dropped as people requested copies of the poster for their conference rooms. Then sometime later, when Jonathan was leading ID&E for Carletta Ooton's HS3C group, there came a formal request from Amazon's Real Estate and Facilities group to have the posters placed in *every* conference room, globally. As the ID&E champion that she is, Carletta sponsored the poster roll-out from her organization's budget. Posters were even translated to local languages in several countries! Amazon is in 1,300+ buildings globally, and each building has, on average, 25 conference rooms. That means the total number of posters was about 32,500. One team dropped one pebble, which led to 32,500 pebbles being dropped. That's a lot of pebbles— enough pebbles to create a massive wave of change. The inclusive meetings tips grew into a daily practice, just as Patti had originally envisioned.

By the way, here are few of our favorite inclusive meeting pebbles to drop:

- Choosing meeting times that optimize attendance across attendee time zones
- Encouraging work owners (as opposed to managers) to present
- Asking others for their opinions or ideas prior to sharing your own
- Setting the expectation that interrupting is disrespectful and prohibited
- Positively calling out inclusive behavior
- Addressing bad behavior in the moment (calling in or calling out)
- Allowing for processing time instead of putting people on the spot

## BUILD A REMOTE CULTURE OF BELONGING

With so many people working remotely, it's easy to lose the personal connection that fosters everyone's sense of belonging. When there is a mixed workforce of remote and in-person employees, it can be particularly difficult to ensure that everyone has the same opportunity to be heard.

When you own a meeting, be sure to set up a conference line or video for the meeting for anyone who can't attend in person. Ensuring that there are multiple ways to attend and participate lets people know that you value their presence and respect the different ways in which they can participate.

In too many hybrid meetings (some people in person, some people virtual), the contributions of video tele-conference (VTC) participants become secondary to the main discussion. Make a habit of intentionally asking for their thoughts and opinions *first* and engaging them throughout the meeting. This is a daily practice that people notice and appreciate, and it is easily replicable. You can even ask one individual in the conference room to help monitor remote participation to ensure their input is included.

It can sometimes be difficult in large hybrid meetings to know exactly who is on the call. Write the names of those on VTC on a whiteboard or place a tent card in the center of the conference room table with all their names so that they stay top of mind.

In group meetings over VTC, it's easy for one or two people to dominate and for other perspectives to be missed. Everyone should have their antennae up to notice whose voice is *not* being heard. Give them the space to speak up without putting any one person on the spot: "Who hasn't had the opportunity to share their thoughts?" or "I'd like to hear from some folks we haven't heard from yet—Jaclyn? Katie? Raj? What do you think?" Encourage people to participate in the way they feel comfortable—whether it's speaking out loud or using the chat function or other features your VTC may offer.

We recommend turning on the closed-captioning feature in your VTC to help everyone follow the conversation, especially when volume levels and accents may inhibit understanding. It's also a good practice to slow down your rate of speech, as it is often challenging to hear the speaker over VTC. Last, it's important to use expressions that are globally understood. Growing your cultural competency will help you be aware of idioms, phrases, and terminology that are culturally specific and not globally well known. Take, for example, such American phrases as "spill the beans," "the cat's out of the bag," and "for the birds."[2] Just as the English speakers' use of idioms is meaningless to non-English speakers, these German, Spanish, and Japanese idioms are meaningless to English speakers. Viewing them here helps you appreciate their visceral experience. Here are some examples: in German, "tomaten auf den Augen haben" (You have tomatoes on your eyes) and "Ich verstehe nur Bahnhof" (I only understand the train station); in Spanish, "Ahogarse en un vaso de agua" (To drown yourself in a glass of water); and in Japanese, 猫の手も借りたい (Willing to borrow a cat's paws).[3]

We recommend whenever possible to have cameras on during virtual meetings. Ask all meeting participants to turn on their cameras, even those in the room with one another. Using video creates a near in-room experience, dissuades people from looking at their phone or email, and encourages full engagement.

We don't recommend making cameras-on mandatory because an inclusive team supports each person's individual decision to do what's best for them to contribute at the highest level. Yet it's key to recognize that in high-context cultures, which more than 60 percent of the world's cultures are, seeing one another's faces makes *everyone* better equipped to "read the air," as Erin Meyer describes in her book *The Culture Map*.[4] Reading the air is your ability to understand what's not being directly stated yet is communicated through the eyes and facial expressions, along with voice tone and inflection. Both low- and high-context communicators benefit when cameras are on to minimize miscommunication.

For those with no visual impairments, seeing people's eyes and at least some body language puts them in a better position to interpret high-context communication, those cues that tell you what the words don't communicate. This is especially valuable in two scenarios: first, during conversations where there is any tension between participants, during discussions of medium- to high-risk topics, and where the outcome has higher stakes; second, when you're on virtual calls with people from across the globe. It's difficult enough trying to create a trusted relationship when you're thousands of miles away from your colleagues. When you can see your coworkers, it does feel as though you're all a bit closer to one another.

Remote work and VTC allow us the ability to bring folks together from all over the world while enjoying greater employee productivity and saving on commuting, real estate, and employee time costs. Whenever possible, we all should take advantage of the benefits provided by the recent massive leap in this technology. With advances in virtual reality, it won't be too long before people will collaborate and interact virtually as if they were in the same room, with even more benefits, including an ideal space for introverts, giving them a manageable way to interact with people that isn't as exhausting as meeting in person.[5]

## SPEND YOUR PRIVILEGE!

Many people face systemic barriers to workplace success through no fault of their own. Spending your privilege is a pebble that helps break down those barriers by your lending a helping hand. Envision the privilege we are talking about as a kind of ordinary privilege—the privilege to forget about aspects of who you are because they represent the majority demographics of our country, community, or organization. You have the power to speak up for those fighting for the respect your ordinary privilege automatically bestows on you. Dolly Chugh, award-winning social psychologist at the NYU Stern School of Business, captured this responsibility beautifully: "For so many of us looking for an opportunity to fight bigotry and bias in the workplace or in our broader culture, we may be missing the opportunity staring back at us in the mirror: using the ordinary nature of who we are as a source of extraordinary power."[6]

As we discussed earlier in the chapter, women are often cut off in meetings and not given the voice to contribute. Men in those situations should speak up, point out what happened, and make it clear they are interested in what the person who has been silenced has to say. This is how they can spend their male privilege in our patriarchal society. The ripples this simple action can generate are clear. First, it codes this behavior as unacceptable and prevents it from becoming a cultural norm. Second, it signals to women that they matter, that people are listening, and that they belong.

Here's another common and easy way to spend your privilege. People in leadership roles who are always asked to speak or meet with other senior leadership can create visibility for others who often don't have that opportunity. Dropping this pebble will signal to others that a diversity of voices is exactly what the organization needs to be better at what it does. It highlights the role of the ally or accomplice in Inclusive Leadership. Spend your privilege, drop a pebble, and have an impact.

## MAKE INTENTIONALITY YOUR DAILY FOCUS

Think of intentionality as conducting actions deliberately with awareness, consciously, and on purpose. As daily practices go, intentionality is a critical guiding principle every inclusive leader needs to embrace. Intentionality, as a philosophical and strategic approach to what leaders focus on in their ID&E work, ensures that they are addressing the most specific and pressing needs in their organizations. A scattershot approach to solving problems often doesn't solve the real problem and is resource intensive. In resource-constrained environments, being intentional allows you to make the most of the dollars, time, and people you have. Intentionality gives you the opportunity to do what is right and not what is expected. This is what Inclusive Leadership looks like!

Intentionality requires the courage to focus on the group with the largest identified gap in representation, retention, or promotion, for example. This could mean creating a retention and engagement program specifically for Black and Latina women in regional roles away from headquarters; in middle management; and with a tenure of less than a year, because that's where the data from a gender demographic assessment showed the largest gap. So now, leaders can target the limited resources they have to solve the biggest issues, enabling them to have the most impact on creating an equitable workplace.

The courage and heart to do what is right and not what is expected comes into play here. Inevitably, people will push back on strategic decisions to roll out a program exclusively for, say, Indigenous and Asian women. They will question whether this is a good use of money (yes), and they will question whether this will, unfairly, give these groups an advantage over, for example, white men or women, or men in general (no). What we have learned from implementing these types of programs is that they ultimately benefit everyone. Closing a representation gap creates a more diverse and creative organization, and what you learn from implementing these programs will help you to be more intentional in how you practice inclusion.

Leading with intentionality means making sure every high-potential employee initiative is created with equity as a criterion. It means questioning, when no one else seems to notice, why the overwhelming majority of a team's lowest-rated employees are Hispanic or Latine. It means making sure every all-hands meeting features a diversity of speakers and particularly speakers from the groups with the least sense of belonging.

# LEAN INTO LEARNING

We often talk about the necessity of *owning* the topic of ID&E. People need to understand what ID&E is for them personally before they can influence or help others. People need to understand how their own lived experiences has shaped who they are and how their perception of who they are and how their various dimensions of diversity influence how they see the world. With this exercise in self-discovery, people can better understand how others see them and are influenced by them. This matters greatly. Each of us needs to own this topic to better understand the impacts of the pebbles we drop and the change we are leading.

Leaning into learning is a critical aspect of the Inclusive Leadership journey. Even advocating for a culture of learning drops the pebble that difference matters, that shared understanding matters, and that ID&E is a strategic imperative as important as any other strategic imperative driving the business.

The beauty of this daily practice lies in just how many ways there are to learn and grow your individual and collective ID&E subject-matter expertise. Carving out five to ten minutes of a staff meeting or an all hands meeting to share something you've learned from a video, an article, or a meaningful conversation you had with someone culturally different is a simple yet powerful pebble to drop. Leaders can hold their teams accountable for spending thirty minutes of their workweek reading an article or watching a video related to ID&E so that they can talk about it. In workplaces where employees don't have desks or access to computers, leaders can take advantage of "daily meeting" group discussions to give an inclusion tip or briefly talk about something they learned in an Inclusive Leadership training.

We are strong advocates for team or organizational ID&E book clubs. Learning collectively and building organizational subject-matter expertise can spark creativity and innovation among stakeholders responsible for solving organization-wide problems.

Taking and advocating for formal, comprehensive Inclusive Leadership training is, in our experience, foundational to developing the knowledge and skills necessary to foster an inclusive workplace environment. If you want a culture of belonging to emerge and flourish, training in what it means to lead inclusively must be an anchor in your overall strategic approach. Openly advocating for and supporting ID&E learning is a must for your journey. Wisdom matters.

## NUDGE ID&E BEHAVIOR

Short, quick, meaningful messages can be effective in drawing the attention of folks toward Inclusive Leadership behaviors. In their 2008 book *Nudge: Improving Decisions about Health, Wealth, and Happiness*, Richard Thaler and Cass Sunstein describe a nudge as "an intervention that gently steers individuals towards a desired action."[7] One of the reasons nudging works with people is that nudges are not mandates; they are suggestions that allow for freedom of choice. Plus, they incur little cost in terms of time or energy.

ID&E nudges can look like short messages, sayings, brief topical learnings, and inspiring "pushes" to do something. They should reinforce people's focus on daily practices by keeping them top of mind. We advocate sending nudges that speak specifically to the different aspects of the employee life cycle or that highlight some important system or structure.

In talent acquisition, for example, a nudge could be an organization-wide email message to all recruiters or hiring managers stating, "Having two women and/or people of color on every interview panel is a powerful branding tool for our organization as a destination employer."

An employee engagement nudge message might be, "Understanding what it means to be an ONLY on a team will help all teammates in building cultures of belonging for everyone."

A development nudge message might be, "Leaning into understanding how we show up in talent management meetings will make an immense difference. Lean in, listen, and learn!"

Establishing ID&E topics as legitimate discussion topics is an important pebble to drop. The ripples from small, impactful messages will spark conversation, reflection, awareness, and behavior change. They may even inspire others to practice nudging. Nudging may even lead to meaningful conversations about unintended messages where an intent versus impact situation happens. This "rocking the boat" may be a needed part of an organization's or team's evolution.

# Chapter 9

# THE HR FUNCTION AS AN ID&E PARTNER

A common challenge organizations face is how to scale ID&E efforts and reach all their employees effectively and equitably. For medium to large companies with global footprints, the practice of integrating ID&E knowledge into the fabric of their people strategy can be daunting in scope. For small companies with a solo ID&E professional on staff—or none at all—doing this work can seem impossible. The solution we have implemented for both of these scenarios is to onboard the HR function as an intentional and active ID&E partner, whether it's your entire HR department, your solo HR person, or the HR consulting company you contract with for your organization.

There is an erroneous belief that HR professionals, by nature of being HR, are automatically ID&E subject-matter experts as they embark on their careers. This assumption has prevented many organizations from appropriately leveraging HR to scale ID&E efforts globally. Organizations need to, intentionally, provide their HR professionals with ID&E training so they can integrate this critical knowledge into how they do their work. The possibilities from doing this are incredible, as we'll explain.

HR professionals touch employees at each stage of the life cycle. They lead talent review meetings, often participate on job candidate interviews, attend leadership staff meetings, review employee rating decisions, investigate harassment or discrimination claims, and are engaged in investigations that lead to an employee being terminated. You get our point. HR professionals are the eyes and ears for all people-related matters. They are also often the only people trusted with an organization's diversity demographic data and the ones tasked to produce those data sets for client meetings, reviews, and discussions. This means that HR professionals are uniquely positioned to drop pebbles across the employee life cycle that can help scale ID&E efforts and create ripples of systemic change.

You can engage with HR to operationalize and scale ID&E work globally. In business lingo, this approach represents a three-legged stool: business units, HR, and ID&E. This simply means that the three are partners in the work, and without one of the players the stool won't work as well. Building a strong ID&E partnership with the HR function, its leaders, and its client professionals will enable ID&E functions, which often have limited resources, to scale throughout an organization. The sad truth is that you need HR to do this work because ID&E teams are, from our experience, woefully underfunded and understaffed. Hearing from our bosses, "You need to find a way to scale your efforts because you aren't getting more (or any) headcount" was our motivation to innovate this way. We used to joke that HR became Eddie's global army as he built out our ID&E strategy.

How this works isn't as big of a lift as it might sound. ID&E teams are already building out learning tools, engagement strategies with business leaders, data assessment strategies and tools, and so on. Simply add to this work an HR partnership component that puts an HR skill-building lens on it. For example, we created an HR-specific version of our Inclusive Leadership training that tweaked the discussions, exercises, and next-step action items to focus exclusively on how HR can incorporate this learning into what they are already doing. We did the same with our demographic data efforts. We held very specific diversity demographic data training for HR professionals to teach them how to assess, analyze, and talk about this data. We even held monthly or bimonthly office hours for HR professionals to drop in with questions, concerns, or simply to increase their subject-matter expertise with diversity data. We also met HR professionals prior to talent management meetings to agree on any key messages, trends, and conversations to be had during these meetings.

With a full understanding of how overwhelmed HR people can be, we didn't require them to add ID&E work to their workload. Instead, we made them full ID&E partners by taking an integrated approach to the work. All of our trainings focused on how ID&E efforts fit into what the HR professionals were already doing and emphasized how we were there for them as partners and accomplices. We showed them the pebbles that will have the biggest ripples and helped them embrace the courage it takes to rock the boat. And yes, we made sure we were true partners and had our hands gripping the boats we expected them to rock!

There is no escaping the reality that HR is everywhere doing people-related work every single day. This partnership ensures that the ripples from your daily practices are spread throughout the organization, influencing the business globally every single day.

From our experience, HR's ID&E work rocked boats and spoke strongly to our shared accountability for these efforts. They signaled to HR professionals everywhere that this work was important and that this message needed to be relayed to their internal business clients. Perhaps the most important ripple we caused with this strategy was the multitude of additional pebbles that were dropped daily throughout the organization and at every level.

## MAKE TALENT INCLUSION ADVOCATE TRAINING MANDATORY

Talent processes and mechanisms such as promotions, reviews and ratings, and succession discussions can accelerate an employees' trajectory or entirely block their growth within an organization. They can serve to either diversify a leadership team or build an impenetrable wall of sameness that could stand for years. The impacts of doing this work wrong are profound, and you need to be able to count on HR professionals to be aware and intentional and to serve as guardians for inclusive talent management. Our experience tells us that there will be boats to rock and plenty of daily practices to deploy before, during, and after these talent management and review processes.

We strongly recommend that HR professionals take a very specific ID&E course on how to be a talent inclusion advocate. Such a course gives precise guidance on how HR needs to show up in these processes, how HR professionals can influence them before, during, and after the completion of the processes, and how they can hold business leaders accountable for their part. We recommend that every business leader who manages people should also take a talent inclusion advocate course.

The pebble you drop as a leader is to charter the creation of a talent inclusion advocate training if it doesn't already exist in your organization. This type of training will trigger innumerable pebbles and ripple effects daily throughout your organization because these processes are being prepared and conducted day in and day out. The ripples this training will cause within the HR function is also an important outcome: ID&E work will be validated daily.

Ripples will play out, for example, in development discussions with employees' managers, or in promotion communications in which employees from underestimated groups see that they matter. For improving talent management process outcomes these are a near silver bullet, especially when rolled out concurrently with robust, intersected data analysis and assessment.

## GIVE HR INTENTIONAL GUIDANCE DURING ID&E TRAININGS

We also recommend creating HR-specific versions of any ID&E training your organization has by simply tweaking the discussions, exercises, and next steps to focus exclusively on how HR professionals can incorporate this learning into what they are already doing and their engagement with internal business clients. Such training literally creates an army of HR professionals who can assist ID&E efforts every single day without doing anything outside their normal roles. What you are enabling is the ongoing dropping of pebbles that make an ID&E perspective and philosophy an integrated, critical component of employee life-cycle work. We found this to be particularly effective with our Inclusive Leadership training at Amazon because this was the primary training we used in Worldwide Operations to help leaders on their Inclusive Leadership journeys. At one point, with the assistance of HR professionals worldwide, we trained over forty thousand employees. What is particularly important to point out, however, is that this number doesn't even account for the countless daily direct connections between HR professionals and business leaders. It was very clear that increasing or enabling HR's capability, via the HR version of Inclusive Leadership training and other ID&E trainings, was invaluable for assisting us in furthering leaders' ID&E journeys.

## MAKE HR PROFESSIONALS DIVERSITY DATA EXPERTS

This daily practice is aimed primarily at leaders in ID&E functions, but is also relevant to business leaders who want to take on this accountability within their organizations. At Amazon, we held very specific diversity demographic data training for HR professionals. It was critical that we didn't assume that just because an HR professional is good with HR people analytics and statistics, they know the kinds of diversity data to ask for, how to assess those data sets, how to help devise gap- and cliff-closing plans, and, important, how to talk about those plans with influence. We even held monthly or bimonthly office hours for HR professionals to drop in with questions and concerns, or to simply increase their subject-matter expertise with diversity data.

The ripples caused from increasing this skill were as impactful as any we can point to. We made sure HR professionals knew how to use diversity data to create irrefutable, and at times eye-popping, arguments about what was needed in a leader's organization and why it mattered. This pebble being dropped daily by HR profoundly rocked boats and was the catalyst for downstream wins with hiring, representation, retention, and development programs.

Making HR professionals a true ID&E partner and an official pebble-dropping machine is a critical global strategy for creating inclusive workplace environments and cultures of belonging. If you stop and reflect on the fact that HR professionals are situated throughout most organizations and are the caretakers for most people-related strategies, then you'll understand that what you can create is the perfect "pebble storm" of systemic change.

Chapter 10

# OVERCOMING HURDLES ON YOUR INCLUSIVE LEADERSHIP JOURNEY

As an inclusive leader, you are going to face resistance on many different fronts during this journey. You simply are not going to get everyone to support your efforts. In fact, if you can get 80 percent of the people to support you, in our experience you're doing great!

Resistance will manifest itself in various ways: getting half the budget dollars requested; receiving no dedicated support from the learning and development team as you try to integrate ID&E into existing training; or hearing perpetual excuses for deprioritizing ID&E program support, the go-to being the crisis du jour. As Roseanne Roseannadanna, one of Gilda Radner's characters on *Saturday Night Live*, would say, "It's always something!"

Sometimes the stumbling blocks are just that. No one is actively trying to sabotage your efforts, but mistakes happen. A smooth road was never promised. Your organization's image or reputation may take a hit through a leader's misguided intent or inappropriate conduct. Bad press can affect your recruiting capabilities and employee retention. Or the company might go through a difficult revenue period with poor financial performance and layoffs that affect the diverse workforce you've worked so hard to grow. If you work for a public company that experiences image-impacting damage due to a public incident or high-profile lawsuit, there can be multiple effects that make your job harder in terms of recruiting and retaining historically marginalized talent.

All of this risk and uncertainty creates hurdles and fatigue that the people doing the good work of ID&E face every day. In this chapter we discuss common hurdles you may face and provide guidance on how to overcome them—or at least to mitigate their impact.

By the way, the first step in overcoming hurdles is to prevent them before they even occur! When we train teams on ID&E using the 2IL model discussed in chapter 2, we advise *slowing down* so they can critically think about why they are making the choices they make. When people move fast, when they are distracted in any way, that's when their decision-making can be affected. Contemplating, slowing things down, and being more introspective are how you develop the wisdom to lead inclusively. Introspection allows you to anticipate hurdles and plan an approach to avoid them or to minimize the damage caused.

Now, let's look at the specific hurdles we've experienced in our careers and how we've learned to manage them.

## RESOURCE CONSTRAINTS

ID&E work is long term and ongoing and has been historically underresourced. Figuring out how to accomplish our goals without the adequate headcount or budget called for creativity, innovation, and passion. Fortunately, we regularly found employees across the companies we worked for who were passionate and committed to ID&E.

Seek out these people in your organization! This is how you build a broad and deep foundational structure for your ID&E program. See chapter 7 for more on how you can provide opportunities for ID&E-committed employees across the organization without adding to their workload. The following is an example of our real-world experience bringing employees into ID&E efforts.

Brad King and Lauren Hruska worked in the Health, Safety, Security, Sustainability, and Compliance (HS3C) group at Amazon, led by ID&E champion VP Carletta Ooton. Eager to get in on the action, Brad and Lauren joined the volunteer-run diversity leadership team and took ownership for the global ID&E Book Club. They helped select the first book, recruited members, earned Carletta's support to fund the books, purchased refreshments for meetings, and gave generously of their time to manage distribution and delivery of the books around the world.

Building grassroots support at all levels across the organization is one of the best ways to overcome the hurdle of resource constraints. When you share the goal of building a culture of belonging with everyone and anyone within earshot, you motivate volunteers to join the journey with you. The success of the ID&E Book Club created momentum for other ID&E projects and programs because even the resisters and skeptics experienced the ripple effect in employee engagement. This is how dropping pebbles creates ripples that become waves. Each success builds on another, making a long-term impact on the work environment.

## PERFORMATIVE DIVERSITY

The organizations that invest in ID&E training, sponsor diversity events, and fly the PRIDE flag each year yet fail to elevate their ID&E strategy to the systems level have a big hurdle to overcome. These companies are doing what many refer to as "performative diversity" without making meaningful progress. As *Forbes* magazine explained,

"[Performative diversity] has the detrimental effect of suppressing attempts to foster genuinely inclusive work environments."[1]

Organizations looking for quick ID&E solutions are seemingly more common now than ever before. With the 2020 murders of Black Americans George Floyd, Breonna Taylor, Ahmaud Arbery, and many, many more in the US, organizations shifted resources to invest in ID&E as a response to the tragedy and global outcry. The pressure caused many leaders to want to present an image of being supportive of equity and justice.

But let's just say outright that publishing an equity statement on your website is not in itself ID&E! If you work with an organization that says it is committed to building a culture of belonging, watch its actions more than its words. Ask challenging questions: What's the multiyear headcount commitment? What's the multiyear annual funding commitment? Are the executives demonstrating ownership and accountability for ID&E results? Whom does the ID&E leader report to? Is your leadership *pulling* for ID&E, or are you in the position of *pushing* ID&E? Are they willing to weave ID&E into everything they do?

To overcome this hurdle, inclusive leaders need to show their organization how it can start creating systemic change today. This is where the daily practices come in. If company leaders are happy with performative diversity because anything more would rock the boat too hard (in terms of resource spend or culture shifts), it is up to inclusive leaders to show them that this work is doable. Change won't happen overnight, but little by little, pebble by pebble, the organization can implement daily practices that strategically build a culture of belonging. It is up to the inclusive leader to show by their words and their actions how to drop pebbles that day by day shift the culture toward one of greater inclusion in a way that is sustainable and works within the rhythm of the business.

# GETTING THE DOMINANT GROUP ON BOARD

Studies going back to the 1950s show that diverse teams outperform homogeneous teams. We know this. The business case for diversity has been proven, time and time again. What has not been communicated well in the past is the role the most privileged groups play in advancing ID&E goals and how they benefit. (As we've noted elsewhere, who constitutes the dominant group varies in different cultures. In the US, white men are the most privileged. In India, there are religious, caste, and gender privileges that manifest in the same way. In too many places, the most privileged are those with the lightest skin color.)

In the US, the unspoken fear of some white men is that ID&E will lead to their replacement by people from historically underrepresented groups. In the media, we hear this expressed as "replacement theory." This fear is often the uncited reason why so many white men push back against the ideals of ID&E.

But ID&E is not a zero-sum game. A rising tide lifts all boats. Increasing diversity of the organization doesn't mean that one group loses and another one wins.

For those in power, explain to them exactly how ID&E helps them. A culture of belonging not only increases performance, creativity, and ultimately innovation throughout the workforce but also makes it easier for leaders to do their jobs! They will have an easier time recruiting and retaining talent because they have the wisdom, heart, and courage to be inclusive of others who are different. They will also have the opportunity to create a "legacy team." In every job they hold thereafter, those employees will yearn to re-create that special culture of team connectedness, that legacy team, the leader built.

Let the members of the dominant group know that you need their diversity of thought and experience too. And you especially need their power, privilege, and status in society to create space for everyone to be seen, heard, valued, and understood. Give them the tools to spend their privilege daily in ways that don't reduce their power but rather grow their respect as inclusive leaders within the organization.

## FEAR OF BACKLASH

In part 1 we outlined the foundational traits of inclusive leaders as wisdom, courage, and heart. We shared that there are leaders who possess wisdom and heart yet lack the courage to act, to put themselves in harm's way for others. This is a hurdle we've seen many times over. Many leaders worry that rocking the boat will jeopardize how they're viewed by others, their advancement opportunities, and their support from management and colleagues. This is very common.

In one company we worked with, there was a director-level leader who purported to be an ally and strong advocate for ID&E in one-to-one meetings—he even rode the company float for the PRIDE parade in Seattle! But he could not muster the courage to speak up in leadership team meetings with his director-level peers and VP to advocate for our ID&E initiatives. At one crucible moment, he failed to stand up for what he believed in. We proposed what is considered the "silver bullet" of ID&E work, candidate slating. His voice in that moment carried the weight to gain broad adoption within the organization. But he sat silent.

To overcome this hurdle, we often coach managers on the characteristics of an ally and accomplice. We give them specific examples of the behaviors we need from them in these crucial moments. When we've worked with similar leaders in-house, we have met informally with them before leadership team meetings to clue them in on the upcoming discussion, tell them precisely what we need them to do, and ask whether they're comfortable doing it. We let them know we need their support and that we will support them in speaking up. We ask for a firm commitment. And when they have followed through, we reinforce their courageous behavior by expressing gratitude and showing them their impact.

## EXCLUSIONARY PRACTICES THAT NOBODY QUESTIONS

This hurdle is about legacy practices that continue to be utilized in a world where they no longer serve any valuable purpose, if they ever did. In many cases, these practices are used either consciously or unconsciously to maintain a workforce that resembles the organization's "founding fathers." They are historical structures, systems, and policies that narrow the pool of applicants while reinforcing and sustaining the power and privilege that are at the core of the socioeconomic chasms in organizations and broader society today. In this section, we'll provide two examples, but many more exist and vary by organization.

*"We only recruit from top-tier schools."*

We've worked for companies that supported strong guidance, in the form of unwritten rules, to only recruit talent from so-called top-tier US schools such as Dartmouth, Harvard, Yale, Stanford, and Carnegie Mellon. These schools are predominantly white, with small populations of Black and Brown students—and they are not the only source of high-caliber candidates.

*"To become a people leader, you must have a degree from a four-year college."*

We worked with a company whose policy was to hire for most corporate roles only people who had at a minimum a four-year undergraduate degree. We know a twenty-plus-year professional who interviewed with the company. Halfway through the hiring process, the interviewer discovered she did not have a four-year degree, and the process was halted. She landed with T-Mobile, and five years later was the chief of staff reporting to the chief human resource officer. While working for T-Mobile, she also earned a bachelor's degree from Arizona State University's Carey School of Business, finishing with a perfect grade-point average of 4.0. Now that's a missed opportunity!

Organizations that have long enjoyed success doing the same things with the same homogenous workforce are less willing to make long-term investments to change the organizational culture. The belief is that what's worked well in the past will propel their future success. The critical point to communicate to these leaders is that holding on to a past where only one type of person with one type of background dominated is an anchor—one that not only prevents the organization from moving forward but also pulls it down and into extinction.

## CULTURE FIT MENTALITY

When a candidate is turned away for not being a "culture fit," the role of an inclusive leader is to ask, What do you mean by "fit"? Often it's code for "this person is different from the organization's cultural norms or exposes a prototype bias."

Next ask, Is what's different about them truly problematic, or just different? Why is it problematic? And if the answer doesn't tie back to the job description or the written set of organizational values, then "fit" is likely being used intentionally or unintentionally as a means of eliminating certain types of people.

Inclusive leaders understand the value of adding people who bring different experiences, ideas, and opinions. This is why we advocate for a "culture-add" mentality rather than one of culture fit. Culture fit is reactive; it leads to stagnation and supports a conformity mindset.

A culture-add mindset is proactive and centered around innovation, and it manifests the value of diversity.

To overcome "They're just not a good fit for our team," hit the pause button, interject, and ask the person to define "fit." Ask the interviewer to give you specifics, because bias lies in the generalities. When leading this conversation, continue to dive deep with follow-up questions to truly understand why the candidate is problematic for the role. There may be a good reason, but to let "fit" go without achieving definitional clarity is to give bias, stereotyping, and potentially ethnocentric behavior free rein.

It might be best to circle back to the fundamental business case for diversity. Teams are jigsaw puzzles, and if all the pieces are the same, it's going to be a very homogenous, uncreative picture! When positions become available on their team, coach leaders to step back and see what pieces of the puzzle are missing. What knowledge, skills, abilities, and perspectives are lacking?

## DISMISSING THE DATA

One of the hurdles we've experienced arises when managers dismiss the data or miss the larger point. Leaders will sometimes push back on ID&E-recommended solutions based on statistical validation arguments. The "small number" issue is a good example. Let's say your job promotion data is critiqued by managers because the large percentage differential between Black women and white women is based on a small sample pool of Black women. The resistance we hear is, "The data pool is too small for this to be considered problematic and doesn't meet statistical significance levels, so we're not taking an action on the identified gap."

Ask those managers to think broadly about the overall experience of Black women in the organization. Explain to them that even in small raw numbers, Black women are not getting promoted as they should be, and the managers need to ask why not. Also ask, And why is the pool of Black women so small in the first place?

If you only have a total of five Black women in an organization and you lose three of them to attrition or transfer, that is in reality a big hit that needs to be addressed. Statistical significance may not be triggered, but you'd better believe that loss will be noticed and have a real impact.

Another circumstance in which pushback can occur is when qualitative data is summarized in reports from interviews or focus groups or ERG discussions, and the conclusions point to issues in the treatment of historically underestimated and marginalized groups. A leader might think that they can dismiss reporting narratives because of their overemphasis on statistical workforce data that isn't indicating an urgent issue—*yet*. In this case, ask the leader to meet directly with a roundtable group of affected employees to hear their stories directly. Get the leader to hear firsthand these employees' lived experience of being passed over, mistreated, or discriminated against. This is a powerful means of getting the leader's attention and support for action. When managers hear the feedback directly, more often than not they believe it.

## CHANGE RESISTERS

Building a culture of belonging is a campaign for organizational change. To be successful, you need to build alliances across the organization to gain the help you need. But what about the people in other departments across the organization? Are any of them resistant to the change you are trying to create? What if they are in a position to make or break your success?

Earlier in the book we discussed understanding each of your team members at a deeper level to create a personal connection. How you create personal connections, particularly with change resisters, is going to vary widely depending on the person you're working with and the context within which you're working. Overall, it's best to take the time to focus on each person individually and to learn what problems they are trying to solve in their business, what keeps them up at night. This helps you to understand how your ID&E work can contribute to helping them solve *their* problems. This is a tie-in to the Platinum Rule, to treat others the way they want to be treated.

What are their individual goals? How can your work help them to be successful in achieving their goals? Reflect; contemplate. Synthesize information to recognize connections, opportunities, options, scenarios. Identify shared goals as you build a trusted relationship. When you help those around you to succeed, and when the work you are doing helps them to succeed, they are more likely to buy in and be a champion for the change you need.

Here are several strategies to influence without authority, to change people's behavior when you do not have the power to direct specific actions:

1. **Leverage existing influence.** Ask leaders who have already bought in to help you influence and win over others. Get them to share the positive business impacts that ID&E is making for them. The more leaders you've got on board, especially trusted leaders, the easier it will be to bring change resisters into the fold.

2. **Communicate other leaders' ID&E successes.** Tapping into people's competitive spirit can be useful for encouraging greater adoption. Show them the results that are drawing the attention of your senior leadership team. If a

change resister's peers are being recognized and rewarded for their success with ID&E, they will not want to be left behind.

3. **Craft compelling stories.** Share with your change resisters the diversity data sets and specific examples from other parts of the organization where ID&E programs are making a real difference.

4. **Center your arguments on the business impacts.** Make sure to show change resisters how ID&E efforts are positively affecting customers, team development, and organizational effectiveness and creativity.

5. **Lead with wisdom, courage, and heart.** Show your skin in the ID&E game. Inspire buy-in by opening up about your energy, passion, and unrelenting belief in ID&E.

For a deeper dive, we recommend Allan R. Cohen and David L. Bradford's management classic, *Influence without Authority*.

## A FOCUS ON COMPLIANCE INSTEAD OF ID&E

There are teams we've worked on where ID&E was a strategy to manage public perception, minimize the risk of lawsuits, or ensure government contract compliance. Organizational leadership would do just enough to appear to be supportive without elevating ID&E to a business imperative. They treated ID&E as a nice-to-have or a compliance requirement rather than as a strategic priority that drives performance, innovation, and profit.

For companies that are government contractors, people can conflate diversity with compliance work. The focus of ID&E is on creating an inclusive, welcoming environment for everyone while leveraging differences to be more creative and innovative in products and services. Compliance is focused exclusively on legal definitions of protected groups for recruiting, hiring, promotion, and retention. There is no law on the books anywhere in any country that says you must have a diversity strategy or hire someone to lead a diversity strategy. But there are legal mandates you must comply with. To do business with the US government, for example, you must have an Affirmative Action program. In South Africa, the relevant law is the Black Economic Empowerment Act. In India, it's known as the Rights for Persons with Disabilities Act, created to support people with disabilities in all spheres of life. ID&E is *not* Affirmative Action, yet it *supports* Affirmative Action compliance as the "good-faith effort" that closes identified gaps.

The best method to overcome this hurdle is education, helping people understand that there is a significant difference between ID&E and compliance. Overall, the latter is limited to a legal responsibility, whereas ID&E serves a broader business imperative, creating a culture of inclusion and belonging.

## FALSE BELIEFS ABOUT MERITOCRACY

A hurdle to Inclusive Leadership and building a culture of belonging is the false belief that the workplace is a pure meritocracy. First coined just over sixty years ago, the term *meritocracy* refers to "the idea that social and economic rewards should track talent, effort, and achievement."[2] It is based on the premise that there is a level playing field and that no one group faces or has faced systemic setbacks to their progress. A belief in meritocracy without understanding the experience of people outside the dominant, majority culture can hamper a leader's ability to lead a diverse workforce.

Part of the problem with meritocracy is its insidious relationship with privilege. According to American feminist, antiracism activist, and scholar Peggy McIntosh, "White privilege is an elusive and fugitive subject. The pressure to avoid it is great, for in facing it, I must give up the myth of meritocracy."[3]

We recently met with the CEO of a 250-person company in the US and asked him to kick off the Inclusive Leadership training course for his people leaders. During our introductory meeting, he shared a story of his father coming to the US at the age of sixteen and how his dad worked to build a very successful life. In short, the lesson from the CEO's story was one of meritocracy. If you studied and worked harder than your competitor, you achieved your goals in life. In that moment, we hit the pause button and shared that his story might fall flat with people in the room who come from communities where they and their parents could not possibly have had the same opportunities simply by studying and working harder than their competitors. This CEO, while having all the positive intent in the world, appeared ignorant of the lived experiences of many communities in this country. For people with inherent power and privilege, his simple advice was true, but for nearly everyone of other races or genders in the US, it is not reality. His beliefs were based on a lack of awareness and knowledge of the many hurdles Black people face in the US in particular, and of many other groups as well. While he had expressed his commitment to equity and inclusion and set the expectation that the company would increase representation of historically underestimated and marginalized people, he perhaps skipped a step to being viewed as a true ally.

To overcome the meritocracy hurdle, ask those who are unwilling to acknowledge their privilege to spend time revisiting what they know about history. Most of us were taught the dominant white culture version of history that left off the stories of those with less power and less privilege. The people in power had the privilege to tell history as they wanted you to know it. We encourage every person reading this book to intentionally relearn the history of your country and the world's cultures through the voices and perspectives of the people who did the hard labor and, in many instances, gave their lives to build the nations of the world. In the US, start with *A Different Mirror: A History of Multicultural America* by Ronald Takaki, which gives a thorough and authentic version of American history that shows America as a country populated and built by diverse peoples from around the world. Another powerful book we recommend is *The 1619 Project: A New Origin Story*, which explores the history of slavery and emancipation in the US and the reverberations we continue to feel today.

These fundamental and deeply ingrained beliefs about meritocracy and privilege are a major hurdle inclusive leaders need to navigate, daily, on their ID&E journeys. We all can chip away at this form of thinking through education and learning. We all can point out the inconsistencies around us. But the reality is that it will take more than poignant comments and supportive illustrative data to get over this hurdle. The challenge is to share experiences where leaders see firsthand the impact of historical and institutionalized oppression, racism, antisemitism, and sexism.

Because this philosophy is so engrained in our society's belief systems, rocking the boat just hard enough to keep others in it may not be enough in every situation. You may need to capsize the boat on occasion. But as daunting as this hurdle can be, have hope. There is power in a consistent wave of ripples from an ever-growing number of inclusive leaders who want to close the gap between our society's stated ideals and the reality that exists for underestimated and marginalized groups. The daily practices of inclusion are how we all get there.

## DIFFERENCES IN VALUES

You may find there are significant chasms between your values as an inclusive leader and the values of the leadership you report to or the colleagues you work alongside. Mining any differences in systemic values will help you understand why you're facing other hurdles that pop up. If you can understand the underlying cause for resistance, you may even be able to anticipate hurdles before they arise. The conversations you have with the leaders around you will inform where you'll be able to progress the culture, how quickly, and with what resources. It's better to go into this work with eyes wide open, knowing what you're going to face so you can plan to manage any adversity. Having multiple conversations with these folks is useful for understanding *why* people hold the values they do. People who identify as part of the dominant majority may feel threatened by ID&E, and your conversations together will go a long way toward your knowing how far you can move them from point A to point B, if at all. From a strategic perspective, there's wisdom in evaluating your tactics for accomplishing your goals—with or without these individuals.

Our experience shows us that some leaders who we were trying to influence weren't always willing participants. Those leaders are rarely going to be transparent and share their values when their beliefs differ from yours. They can pose the most dangerous of all hurdles because they will be covert in their undermining your ID&E efforts, either consciously or unconsciously. They may view you as a competitive threat to their work because you shift the focus away from their team's priorities. They may act in the name of protecting budgets and headcount. Yet over time their behavior unveils their values.

What you will most frequently encounter are subtle, often unconscious defensive postures. Perhaps these people refuse to meet with you or continually cancel meetings or not show up at all, for example.

Perhaps they decide they don't have the capacity to work on a goal driven by a team or person outside of their team. But pretty quickly these folks will show their stripes through their actions more than their words. Their microinsults (sometimes not so micro), false narratives, or invalidations will reveal whom you're working with and what you're up against.

One memorable example was of a leader who repeatedly complained that the diversity data didn't look right (though it was accurate) and was unwilling to initiate any ID&E projects until the data was corrected to her satisfaction. This same leader would schedule her organization-wide diversity training yet not stay for the session or, in another instance, would join the training yet leave regularly to take phone calls.

Another very senior leader in the same division complained that the CEO wasn't doing enough to support diversity and used that as an excuse for not supporting the work in her own organization. She complained that there weren't enough people of color on the senior leadership team; therefore, the CEO was not supportive of ID&E and therefore she would not support it either—a highly flawed argument. We should acknowledge here that some people do become legitimately overwhelmed by the immutability of the status quo, especially if they are part of the nondominant group. A response of this nature could be a telling sign of how broken things are. In general, however, such excuses are red herrings. They come from managers who support diversity efforts in theory, but are unwilling to do the actual work, who act in ways that either contradict their vocalized values or sabotage the ID&E efforts of others.

As an ID&E champion, you need to understand the environment you are working in so that you can implement strategies to bring people with different values on board. We mention a few in the "Change Resisters" section of this chapter. But you also need to know when to cut your losses. When you're digging for treasure, you can only dig for so long and go so deep before acknowledging that there's nothing there and it's time to dig in a new spot. No matter how persistent and creative you might be in trying to win people over, you must at some point recognize that some change resisters aren't going to change. Invest your time where there's the potential for adoption of ID&E values despite the detractors.

Who are the managers and employees who are willing to roll up their sleeves and become actively involved in the day-to-day work? These leaders prioritize ID&E, show up to ID&E meetings and events consistently, model the behavior they expect of their peers, and drop pebbles with regularity. Your time and resources are finite too, so prioritize, prioritize, prioritize. Spend time where you can get the most traction, do the most good, and make the biggest impact. Find the treasure!

## THINKING THE WORK HAS ALREADY BEEN DONE

This hurdle is often difficult to address. If you are dealing with a leader, team, or organization that is convinced they are aware, equitable, and clearly without any ID&E issues to speak of, how can you convince them that there's still work to be done? False confidence can result in blinders that obscure critical ID&E gaps, cliffs, and needs.

Sometimes this confidence comes from a place of idyllic ignorance. People might truly feel that they have the resources in place and the programs running, and, in their minds, there is no way anyone is being treated unfairly. The conversations with leaders who are happily ignorant tend to be difficult, but showing them really good intersected data (if it exists) is an excellent way to begin chipping away at their false perceptions. If great data doesn't exist, we've found that taking leaders on listening tours with underestimated and marginalized groups can be eye opening. Poignant employee testimonials can do the trick as well.

By contrast, conversations with leaders who are entrenched in their beliefs will bring an entirely different set of challenges. The aforementioned tactics are worth trying. However, realize that it will take far more effort and time to move someone away from culturally pervasive meritocratic mental model that reinforces the belief that they have earned what they have, that if you work hard, you will be successful no matter what, and that the cream always rises to the top.

The closest thing to a silver bullet that we've seen in these cases is a sudden personal revelation or life experience that challenges the core of the person's beliefs. For example, we've seen dozens of male leaders have a very sudden change in entrenched beliefs when their wives or daughters experienced discrimination that was far from objective, meritocratic, or fair. It took a personal, emotional, and close-to-home experience for them to join us on our inclusion journey with equity as the end point.

This particular hurdle is often overlooked, and addressing it requires a willingness to challenge deep cultural beliefs. You must be ready to willingly and intentionally rock boats hard and weather denial, dismissive behaviors, and, if you lead ID&E efforts, challenges to the necessity of your role. This is where wisdom, heart, courage, and a deep conviction for doing what is right and not what is expected come in handy.

## PUSHBACK AGAINST INTENTIONALITY

If, for example, your data indicates that military veterans as a group have a promotion velocity three times slower than other groups regardless of employee rating, there is a clear bias at play. What's indicated to address this data-supported assessment is an intentional program exclusively for veterans. An effective program could set accelerated promotional targets, establish a mentoring program with senior leaders as mentors, require all managers of military veterans to work with these employees to create career development plans, then be accountable to leadership for explaining why a target is missed.

We encourage you to develop and execute intentional programs like this, but be ready for pushback. You will face different levels of resistance depending on where your intentionality takes you. Programs for intentionally closing a racial gap seem to face the most resistance.

You may face resistance from leaders who lack the wisdom or courage to support the rollout of an intentional program because they fear the pushback they would get from the majority members on their team. Your lawyers might be worried about the legal risk of such programs. Some leaders will be the ones pushing back directly: if they have a dogmatic meritocratic mindset, they may see these types of programs as giving undue advantage to one group over another, what they might call "reverse discrimination." They cite fairness for all and fail to acknowledge the unintentional and intentional barriers that underestimated and marginalized groups face every day. We've had this very discussion too many times to count, unfortunately.

But here's the simple truth. Intentional programs, if successful, ultimately benefit everyone in an organization. Everyone. So not only are you able to close some of the identified diversity workforce gaps, but the key programmatic learnings can be used broadly to benefit all employees. This is a win-win situation. Another beneficial ripple of the intentionality pebble is the impact on the underestimated and marginalized groups on whom you purposefully focused. When people feel seen and leadership puts real resources and energy into creating an inclusive workplace, they are more likely to stay, be more engaged, and recommend the company to other underestimated or marginalized folks.

Inclusive leaders fight against intentionality pushback by showing how the results of these programs have organization-wide benefits. They provide examples of intersected data that explicitly demonstrate how closing the gap on a particular situation will have ripple effects throughout the workforce. They share stories and testimonials about how the program makes people in the targeted group feel seen. This alone has positive downstream impacts on retention, engagement, and the belief that the leadership cares about these individuals' well-being and place in the organization.

## DIVERSITY FATIGUE

For ID&E leaders and champions, a common phrase often applies: "diversity fatigue." We often tell folks doing this work that ID&E is a marathon—maybe even an ultramarathon!—not a sprint. The effort requires a multiyear commitment, and sustainable change does not take place overnight. The journey of building a culture of belonging is not a direct line from a starting point to an accomplished goal. It's closer to the travels of a pinball from the top of the machine to the bottom—a circuitous trip, popping around, getting bumped from here to there, until the ball finally reaches its destination. The long, circuitous journey can be debilitating at times, and it will require resilience and creativity for you to keep on dropping pebbles.

As an inclusive leader working to build a culture of belonging, you will need to fill your boat's storage compartment with plenty of wisdom, heart, and courage—and a laser focus on the goal. No matter the obstacles you face, never lose sight of the vision you have of the future. A deep conviction for doing what is right and not what is expected will come in handy.

# Conclusion

# CHALLENGE ACCEPTED!

## *What It Means to Lead Inclusively*

There is an undeniable relationship between consistent daily practices of Inclusive Leadership and building a culture of belonging. For this reason, we challenge you to integrate these practices into your daily work life.

We've joked over the years that leading inclusively and ID&E work in general aren't rocket science . . . most of the time. But they can be complicated and challenging simply because humans are involved. That's why we dedicated a whole chapter to overcoming hurdles!

What we've tried to do in this book is take the pressure off of doing this work. Practicing inclusion doesn't mean being perfect—no one is or can be. But it does mean striving to do the right thing every day, dropping pebbles every day, walking the talk, and holding yourself and others accountable.

In *An American Dilemma*, author Gunnar Myrdal wrote that too many people wake up every day ignoring the fact that a stark contradiction is staring them in the face. Subsequently, they fail to act.[1] The contradiction in the US is the disturbing discrepancy between the country's creed of respect for inalienable rights to freedom, justice, and opportunity for all and the pervasive realities of discrimination, harassment, and oppression. But the US is not alone. Most other countries have their own dilemmas and contradictions that too many people are willing to ignore. Too many just don't care enough to wrestle with this dilemma and do something about it, even something small. As inclusive leaders, we all must challenge ourselves to have a dilemma about what is happening around us and to do something about it. It means having a dilemma when things aren't inclusive and equitable. Every day!

Deep down in their hearts, inclusive leaders know they need to do something about the lack of fairness, access, inclusion, and belonging for marginalized groups. This is where daily practices of Inclusive Leadership come into play. These practices pave the way for you to bring your whole self to leadership. Consistently applied daily practices lead to tangible outcomes of leaders embracing a mindset of inclusion and rocking the boat when necessary and as hard as required. Without this mindset, it will take way too long to close the gaps historically underestimated and marginalized groups are attempting to cross—gaps caused by systemic and structural dynamics that have resulted in generations of unearned advantages for majority groups.

The cool thing about a daily practice is that it never becomes so daunting that you shut down or, worse yet, resist. Inclusive leaders understand that they don't need to overwhelm themselves trying to push the proverbial boulder up the hill. They understand the power of intentionally dropping a pebble that causes a ripple that causes someone else to drop a pebble, which causes another ripple, and so on. They have the wisdom to know which pebbles to drop, the ones that will cause ripples in their teams and business units and eventually lead to waves of system-wide change in their entire organization. There is power in knowing that the aggregation of all those intentional pebbles leads to sustainable systemic and cultural change.

By the way, one of the most important pebbles you can drop is to hold your team accountable for dropping their own pebbles. That's what leads to the ripple effect. The image that should come to mind is of change occurring from the top down, the middle out, *and* the bottom up.

Throughout this book, we've offered up a lot of proven daily practices. Our intent was not to provide an exhaustive list, however. No way! Rather, our goals were to illustrate what is possible when you have a daily practice of inclusion and to inspire a sense in all of us that amazing things are within our grasp when we embrace the wisdom, heart, and courage it takes to lead inclusively.

Our challenge to all readers is that you need to have a dilemma. Globally, people are not living up to aspirations of equity and belonging. We challenge everyone to find the courage to rock boats and rock them hard. We challenge everyone to drop ripple-causing pebbles that generate waves of change everywhere—workplaces, communities, families, and, perhaps idealistically, the world.

## GUIDING PRINCIPLES FOR LEADING INCLUSIVELY

Inclusion is a system rich with complexity, and we acknowledge that there is an interplay between the 2IL model, the daily practices, and the guiding principles we outline in this chapter. These guiding principles give you the credibility you need to be believed, trusted, and followed as an inclusive leader. They give your daily practices of inclusion meaning both for yourself and for others. As we have argued throughout our book, your ID&E efforts don't need to be overwhelming, daunting, or complicated. They need to be thoughtful, intentional, authentic, and consistent. We encourage you to embrace this interplay in these last few pages. Personally, these guiding principles have made our own Inclusive Leadership journeys more meaningful and exciting. We hope they will act as catalysts facilitating your ability to act, just as they have for us.

## Make It Your Own

While at Microsoft, we were fortunate to have an executive coach who advised us on how to be more effective leaders. This coach recommended blocking out two hours a week for "white space." White space is dedicated time away from the people and the work. It is a set period for personal reflection to contemplate and to gain perspective. The value of white space can be immense, facilitating greater clarity of thought, the generation of innovative ideas and different ways of thinking about anything related to work or one's broader life. We hope this book provides white space for you to own what Inclusive Leadership means in your daily work life.

Right now, before you do anything else, reflect on the seven insights of the 2IL model. Make this topic, this practice, and this journey your own. How have the insights influenced your experience in the workplace and the experiences of others? Revisit chapter 2 if need be, and keep on going back to it. There is no more direct path to ID&E wisdom than owning the insights described in the 2IL model. Understand the model for sure, but also challenge yourself to reflect on how the key concepts—inclusion, diversity, equity, intersectionality, and so on—figure into your own life. Own the understanding that systems and systemic thinking are key, that life cycles are not individual stages but interconnected threads in the 3D sphere that is the employee experience.

## Lead with Intentionality

"You do not rise to the level of your goals. You fall to the level of your systems." These are some wise words from James Clear, the bestselling author of *Atomic Habits*.[2] We should all challenge ourselves to be intentional about affecting systems, processes, and structures. Doing so will prevent us from practicing performative ID&E that has very little impact on structural or cultural change. Performative ID&E often leads to one-off changes that are not sustainable or particularly impactful. We all need to push ourselves to do intentional work that addresses the belief systems such as racism, antisemitism, sexism, and meritocracy that prevent real change from happening. This is how inclusive environments are created and how belonging gets its foundation.

Think of intentionality as deliberately, purposefully, and strategically dropping pebbles of inclusion. This takes wisdom, heart, and the courage to rock boats when needed. One example of intentional leadership would be to develop a program specifically designed to close a gap in the representation of Black and Brown women in senior-level roles. More broadly, it can be making each of your SMART goals SMARTIE goals instead, by ensuring that whatever you achieve has a positive impact on inclusion and equity. (For a refresher on SMARTIE goals, see chapter 7.) This is how you lead intentionally and hold yourself accountable for true impact.

Meaningful and sustainable impact results from seeing where you can create change systemically, not in silos. We challenge you to see the threads that tie together talent acquisition, development and management, retention, and engagement. Be intentional about dropping pebbles that impact these critical points in the life cycle of an employee.

## Make Equity the End Game

Many of us wrestle with notions of equal opportunity, equality, and equity. Equal-opportunity thinking excludes the possibility of any external influences—for example, sexism, racism, systemic oppression, conscious or unconscious bias, microaggressions, and other barrier-raising dynamics. Equality means treating everyone exactly the same, despite the simple truth that everyone is not the same. It ignores the reality that for many, a one-size-fits-all approach is not fair. Equity recognizes that fairness doesn't mean that everyone gets the same thing but that everyone gets what they need to be successful. Equity and access are more than just having a seat at the table; they are having a voice and being heard by everyone at the table. We challenge you to make equity your end game.

## Embrace Empathy to Get to Belonging

Inclusive leaders understand that the gateway to inclusion is empathy and that belonging results from their personal and organizational inclusion efforts. Empathy isn't about putting yourself in someone else's shoes or believing you can feel their pain. It is showing respect and genuine interest in the realities of others who are different from you. When you truly acknowledge the barriers, oppression, systemic exclusion, and discrimination the other person experiences, you will begin to empathize with them. And you need empathy to be authentic in your daily practice of inclusion. The other components of heart—having compassion and being vulnerable—are accelerants in this equation, especially in how you model inclusion.

It is also important to remember that acts of inclusion and a sense of belonging are two different things. Inclusion is the work you personally do or the efforts an organization advocates. Belonging is what people feel as a result of inclusion efforts. Belonging is solidified when people feel they have a voice and are heard.

## Keep It Simple

Inclusive leaders know that doing this work doesn't require huge, Sisyphean efforts pushing boulders up a hill. A good way to conceptualize what is needed is to think about an airplane in flight. If you want to change directions, you don't want to suddenly bank hard to the left or right. That is jarring, can be scary, and feels out of control. What you do is gradually, a degree at a time, bank in the direction you want to go. One degree at a time, one pebble at a time . . . before long you will have changed directions and be heading on a new course.

## Spend Your Privilege

Inclusive leaders spend their ordinary, everyday privilege to help others who face barriers, oppression, and marginalization. Think of ordinary privilege this way: most of us don't need to consider certain aspects of who we are (race, gender, religion, physical ability, and so on) because they represent the majority demographics of our country, organization, or community. Others from historically underestimated groups cannot count on having this privilege, and this is an extra burden they must bear through no fault of their own. Inspired by Peggy McIntosh's essay called "White Privilege: Unpacking the Invisible Knapsack," Barry Deutch, in his article "The Male Privilege Checklist" wrote a powerful statement that has stuck with us about the responsibility of those with ordinary privilege: "The first big privilege which whites, males, people in upper economic classes, the able bodied, the straight (I think one or two of those will cover most of us) can work to alleviate is the privilege to be oblivious to privilege."[3] Challenge yourself to use whatever privilege you have to help others. This can be as simple as speaking up for those who don't have the luxury of being oblivious to who they are.

## Remember the Danger of the Single Story

Recognize the importance of power in determining whether a single story or a balance of stories defines the person, culture, country, or company. As we discussed in chapter 1, adopting a single story that show a people as one thing and only one thing ultimately leads to their becoming that single story. That single story forces us to overlook the many other stories that would help us understand who they are in deeper, nonstereotypical or unbiased ways.

## Listen to Their Stories

Even though you are doing intentional ID&E work and are focused on creating a workplace environment that fosters the sense of belonging, that might not be enough for some. There very well might be people who feel so marginalized that no matter what their organization does to be inclusive, they have no hope of ever getting over the barriers that confront them every day. Your challenge here is to listen. Seek out those who don't feel included and listen to their stories. Acknowledge their experiences and their stories, and show you are there to listen and to learn from them. Be empathetic and make them feel heard.

## Find Your Voice and Use It

The social dynamics in meetings or during any variety of interactions influence how comfortable people feel about speaking up when they hear or see something wrong. There is a great video called "That Little Voice" that we use to challenge leaders to speak up when they see something discriminatory, even when it is daunting or uncomfortable to do so.[4] "That Little Voice" clearly illustrates how anyone can fail to speak up in situations where someone is the target of sexist, racist, homophobic, and other demeaning behaviors. It also makes it clear that anyone can be a target of this behavior. The video shows people finding the courage to speak up, and challenges viewers to do the same. We echo this challenge and strongly urge everyone to speak up for others in whatever way is most comfortable. It is that important.

Being comfortable with your discomfort is a sign of growth in the ID&E space, so we encourage everyone to speak up even if it is uncomfortable. When you, as a leader, do this, you model what it's like to be a part of a speak-up culture, which is essential to creating belonging. We encourage people at all levels, in all roles, in all geographies, and across the spectrums of diversity dimensions to feel empowered to speak up for themselves and others. (Chapter 8 provides several related daily practices, including assuming positive intent, calling in and calling out, and hitting the pause button.)

## NOTHING CHANGES IF NOTHING CHANGES

There is a funny comic strip with two men, probably white, sitting together at lunch. One man says to the other, "On the way to lunch, I listened to a hip-hop station on the car radio. I believe that satisfies our cultural diversity requirement for another year." We strongly and adamantly do *not* want to be anyone's hip-hop station. We hope that after reading this book, you feel compelled and inspired to do something different, to drop pebbles, to hold others accountable for doing the same, for having a dilemma. Because nothing changes if nothing changes.

We've purposefully framed our book around the wisdom, heart, and courage to lead inclusively, to practice daily inclusion, and to drop the pebbles that cause ripples of change. This is how you create a culture of belonging. The wisdom you garner because of your shared understanding of ID&E makes the steps you take on your journey impactful. Your heart is the catalyst that sparks your ability to act on what you've learned and experienced. Heart is waking every day with the dilemma that barriers exist and something needs to be done about them. Your courage is what ensures that what you do about the dilemma is meaningful, wide reaching, and sustainable. Courage enables you to continually drop the pebbles that will eventually rock the boat and rock it hard.

Throughout the book, we've zeroed in on how to practice inclusion daily and at every stage of the employee life cycle. We've discussed the need to address structure and accountability, talent acquisition (attract), and talent management (develop, keep, and engage). We put a special spotlight on HR professionals as true ID&E partners. We've also, we hope, made it clear that you aren't expected to do this alone. You need to hold those around you—your direct reports, teams, and colleagues—accountable to play their part in being tempered radicals, dropping pebbles, and striving to lead inclusively.

Do the math. If you encourage ten people to drop pebbles that cause ripples, which inspires ten more people to drop pebbles that cause ripples, which inspires ten more people to do the same, the aggregation of these efforts can create a tidal wave of impact that starts small and grows into a remarkable force for change.

The outcome of all of this—dropping pebbles, rocking boats, practicing daily inclusion—is the creation of a culture of belonging that becomes the catalyst for creativity and innovation. When *all* people feel that they have a voice, are authentically heard, and truly are a part of a company's vision, then the sky is the limit. All of us simply need to embrace the wisdom, heart, and courage it takes to make this a reality. One pebble at a time. One ripple at a time. One daily practice at a time.

As we briefly discussed in the introduction, there is a meaningful current topic about which we'd be remiss if we didn't address it. There continues to be a global attack on programs and the people working for progress on inclusion, equity, and justice. In the US, we've experienced, for example, the purposeful whitewashing of history in Florida, book banning in multiple states, an outrageous onslaught of hate aimed at LGBTQ communities, overt actions to limit voting and to further disenfranchise Black and Brown Americans, a historic increase in antisemitism and Asian hate crimes, and the decimation of women's right to choose what they do with their own bodies. We've even seen the country's highest court use race-blind ideology to overturn Affirmative Action in our far from race-blind colleges and universities. This is only a partial picture of all the incredibly damaging actions under way, and the organizations in which we all work are not immune. There have been increasing attacks against ID&E efforts in the workplace that we fear will quickly escalate beyond Affirmative Action to the dismantling of ID&E as a function. Folks, we have a dilemma.

The current sociopolitical climate means that it is time to double down on ID&E. We all need to ramp up our wisdom, heart, and courage to prepare for the tsunami of backlash that is on us. We all need to continue arguing for the irrefutable ID&E business case and the empirically confirmed relationship between ID&E efforts and global innovation and creativity. We all need to emphasize the importance of creating access to jobs, processes, and programs while clearly pointing out that this is in no way creating an advantage or disadvantage. These efforts are about reflecting our communities and customers and, again, making business solutions more global, inclusive, and innovative.

Facing this dilemma will be overwhelming and frustrating and downright scary at times. But we can say, with certainty, that if we all don't galvanize around what we've talked about in our book and all the other wonderful ID&E work that is out there, society risks losing so very much. Too much. We all could lose any hope for cultures of belonging, for equity and social justice, for dismantling institutionalized discrimination and oppression. This may sound overly dramatic, but we strongly believe that hope is being threatened. Period.

Our final challenge then is for all of us to have a dilemma that sparks action, to rock boats and rock them hard, and to not only push accountability out to others but compassionately and courageously face these attacks on what we do and who we are.

# Notes

## INTRODUCTION

1. Debra E. Meyerson, *Tempered Radicals: How People Use Difference to Inspire Change at Work* (Boston: Harvard Business School Press, 2001).

2. Alan Feuer, "White Supremacist Propaganda Soared Last Year, Report Finds," *New York Times*, March 9, 2023, https://www.nytimes.com/2023/03/09/us/politics/white-supremacist-propaganda.html; Lisa Deaderick, "New Conversations Defining 'Terrorism' Need to Include White Supremacist Violence," *San Diego Tribune*, May 21, 2023, https://www.sandiegouniontribune.com /columnists/story/2023-05-21/new-conversations-defining-terrorism-need -to-include-white-supremacist-violence.

3. Brandon Girod, "Florida Has Banned Nearly 400 Books in Schools. Here's the Full List," *Pensacola News Journal*, September 22, 2023, https://www .pnj.com/story/news/education/2023/09/22/florida-leads-nation-in-book -bans-full-list-of-banned-books/70934406007/; Brian Lopez, "Texas Has Banned More Books Than Any Other State, New Report Shows," *Texas Tribune*, September 19, 2022, https://www.texastribune.org/2022/09/19/texas -book-bans/.

4. Shawna Mizelle, "Lawmakers in 32 States Have Introduced Bills to Restrict Voting So Far This Legislative Session," CNN, February 22, 2023, https://www.cnn.com/2023/02/22/politics/restrict-voting-bills-introduced -us/index.html; Richard L. Hasen and Dahlia Lithwick, "The Effort to Suppress the Vote Is Spreading to the Republican Mainstream," *Slate*, April 11, 2023, https://slate.com/news-and-politics/2023/04/republican-effort-to -suppress-the-vote.html; Janie Boschma, Fredreka Schouten, and Priya

Krishnakumar, "Lawmakers in 47 States Have Introduced Bills That Would Make It Harder to Vote. See Them All Here," CNN, April 3, 2021, https://www.cnn.com/2021/04/03/politics/state-legislation-voter-suppression/index.html.

5. Hassan Kanu, "U.S. Supreme Court Enabled Racial Gerrymandering in South Carolina," Reuters, January 17, 2023, https://www.reuters.com/legal/government/us-supreme-court-enabled-racial-gerrymandering-south-carolina-2023-01-17/; Andrew Witherspoon and Sam Levine, "These Maps Show How Republicans Are Blatantly Rigging Elections," *Guardian,* November 12, 2021, https://www.theguardian.com/us-news/ng-interactive/2021/nov/12/gerrymander-redistricting-map-republicans-democrats-visual.

6. Randall, "Hate Crimes against Asian Americans Surge, FBI Reports," *AsAmNews,* March 27, 2023, https://asamnews.com/2023/03/27/updated-report-corrects-underreporting-bias-crimes/.

7. "Discrimination Experiences Shape Most Asian Americans' Lives," November 30, 2023. https://www.pewresearch.org/race-ethnicity/2023/11/30/asian-americans-and-discrimination-during-the-covid-19-pandemic/.

8. Theara Coleman, "America's Alarming Rise in Antisemitism," *The Week,* March 27, 2023, https://theweek.com/crime/1022048/americas-alarming-rise-in-antisemitism.

9. "ADL Center on Extremism Notes Nearly 400-Percent Increase in Preliminary Antisemitic Incidents Reported Year Over-Year," October 24, 2023. https://www.adl.org/resources/press-release/adl-records-dramatic-increase-us-antisemitic-incidents-following-oct-7.

10. Fabiola Cineas, "History Repeating Itself": How the Israel-Hamas war Is Fueling Hate Against Muslims and Jews," October 31, 2023. https://www.vox.com/23930119/hate-crimes-muslims-jews-palestinians-arabs-fear.

## PART 1

1. Martin Luther King Jr., James Melvin, and Coretta Scott King, *I Have a Dream: Writings and Speeches That Changed the World* (New York: HarperCollins Publishers, 1992).

# CHAPTER 1

1. Chimamanda Ngozi Adichie, "The Danger of a Single Story," TED, July 2009, https://www.ted.com/talks/chimamanda_ngozi_adichie_the_danger_of_a _single_story?language=en.

# CHAPTER 2

1. Corin Ramos and Sheila Brassel, *Intersectionality: When Identities Converge* (New York: Catalyst, 2020).
2. Amanda Enayati, "The Importance of Belonging," CNN, October 24, 2023. https://www.cnn.com/2012/06/01/health/enayati-importance-of-belonging/ index.html.
3. Adetoun Yeaman and Sreyoshi Bhaduri, "Empathy: The First Step towards Inclusion," *All Together*, July 14 2020, https://alltogether.swe.org/2020/07/em pathy-first-step-towards-inclusion/.
4. Jeremy Kirk, "Zune Another Kind of Four-Letter Word in Hebrew? Microsoft Zune: Doesn't Sound Sweet to Everyone," *Computerworld*, October 20, 2006, https://www.computerworld.com/article/2547634/zune-another-kind-of -four-letter-word-in-hebrew-.html.
5. John Flinn, "Microsoft Employees Were Arrested in Turkey after a Software Map Showed Kurdistan to Be a Separate Entity," *Ekurd Daily*, December 19, 2004, https://ekurd.net/mismas/articles/misc/turkeymicrosoft.htm.
6. Project Implicit, n.d., accessed July 22, 2023, https://implicit.harvard.edu/im plicit/takeatest.html.
7. Derald Wing Sue, *Microaggressions in Everyday Life: Race, Gender, and Sexual Orientation* (Hoboken, NJ: Wiley, 2010).

# CHAPTER 3

1. Anne Ju, "Courage Is the Most Important Virtue, Says Writer and Civil Rights Activist Maya Angelou at Convocation," *Cornell Chronicle*, May 24, 2008, https://news.cornell.edu/stories/2008/05/courage-most-important-virtue -maya-angelou-tells-seniors.

## CHAPTER 4

1. John C. Maxwell, *The 21 Irrefutable Laws of Leadership*, 25th anniv. ed. (Nashville, TN: HarperCollins Leadership, 2022).

## CHAPTER 5

1. Kate Gautier and Lalith Munasinghe, "Build a Stronger Employee Referral Program," *Harvard Business Review*, May 26, 2020, https://hbr.org/2020/05/build-a-stronger-employee-referral-program.
2. Alexandra Carter, "3 Examples of Great Diversity Employee Referral Programs," *OnGig* (blog), September 12, 2021, https://blog.ongig.com/diversity-and-inclusion/diversity-employee-referral-programs/.
3. Greg Lewis and Manas Mohapatra, "The Most In-Demand Jobs on LinkedIn Right Now," *LinkedIn Talent Blog*, November 2, 2023, https://www.linkedin.com/business/talent/blog/talent-strategy/most-in-demand-jobs.
4. Janice Gassam Asare, "What Is White Saviorism and How Does It Show Up in Your Workplace?" *Forbes*, September 30, 2022, https://www.forbes.com/sites/janicegassam/2022/09/30/what-is-white-saviorism-and-how-does-it-show-up-in-your-workplace/.
5. "Beth Galetti's Post," LinkedIn, n.d., accessed July 21, 2023, https://www.linkedin.com/feed/update/urn:li:activity:6386621037114724352/.

## CHAPTER 6

1. Stefanie K. Johnson, David R. Hekman, and Elsa T. Chan, "If There's Only One Woman in Your Candidate Pool, There's Statistically No Chance She'll Be Hired," *Harvard Business Review*, April 26, 2016, https://hbr.org/2016/04/if-theres-only-one-woman-in-your-candidate-pool-theres-statistically-no-chance-shell-be-hired.
2. "Candidate Interview and Employer Brand Report," Greenhouse, Q3 2022, 4, https://assets.website-files.com/62fe5b1f1365fa2c2a244b0e/631a45d855bf9c61227515ef_Greenhouse-candidate-culture-survey-Sept-2022.pdf.
3. "Diverse Representation Framework & Diverse Interview Panels," Cisco, n.d., accessed July 31, 2023, https://www.ceoaction.com/actions/diverse-representation-framework-diverse-interview-panels/.
4. Katherine Reynolds Lewis, "Diverse Interview Panels May Be a Key to

Workplace Diversity," tvmc, June 16, 2016, https://www.vernamyers.com
/2017/06/16/diverse-interview-panels-may-be-a-key-to-workplace-diversity/.

## CHAPTER 7

1. Jessica Gingrich, "The Underground Kitchen That Funded the Civil Rights Movement: Georgia Gilmore's Cooking Fueled the Montgomery Bus Boycott," Atlas Obscura, December 21, 2018, https://www.atlasobscura.com/articles /who-funded-civil-rights-movement.
2. "The Truest Eye: On the Greater Good," Oprah.com, https://www.oprah.com /omagazine/toni-morrison-talks-love/4.
3. "Microsoft Instructed All Workers to Set Diversity Goals in Performance Reviews. Employees Taking Optional DEI Courses Increased by 270%," Yahoo Finance, November 9, 2023, https://finance.yahoo.com/news/micro soft-instructed-workers-set-diversity-160941472.html.
4. Allen Smith, "More Companies Use DE&I as Executive Compensation Metric," SHRM, July 12, 2021, https://www.shrm.org/resourcesandtools/legal-and -compliance/employment-law/pages/dei-as-executive-compensation-metric .aspx.

## CHAPTER 8

1. Robert Holden, "I See You! Are You Also Looking at Me?" Heal Your Life, July 26, 2011, https://www.healyourlife.com/i-see-you.
2. Zoë Miller and Frank Olito, "25 phrases Americans say that leave foreigners completely stumped," Insider, December 28, 2019, https://www.insider.com /confusing-things-americans-say-2018-4.
3. Helene Batt and Kate Torgovnick May, "40 Brilliant Idioms That Simply Can't Be Translated Literally," TED Blog, January 20, 2015, https://blog.ted .com/40-idioms-that-cant-be-translated-literally/.
4. Erin Meyer, The Culture Map: Breaking through the Invisible Boundaries of Global Business (New York: PublicAffairs, 2014).
5. Thomas Griffin, "Why VR Is an Innovative Way to Think about Remote Meetings," Forbes, March 30, 2020, https://www.forbes.com/sites/forbestech council/2020/03/30/why-vr-is-an-innovative-way-to-think-about-remote -meetings/?sh=691507993370.

6. Dolly Chugh, "Use Your Everyday Privilege to Help Others," *Harvard Business Review*, September 18, 2018, https://hbr.org/2018/09/use-your-everyday-privilege-to-help-others.

7. Richard H. Thaler and Cass R. Sunstein, *Nudge: Improving Decisions about Health, Wealth, and Happiness* (New York: Penguin Group, 2008)

## CHAPTER 10

1. "Performative Allyship: What Are the Signs and Why Leaders Get Exposed," *Forbes*, November 26, 2020, https://www.forbes.com/sites/carmenmorris/2020/11/26/performative-allyship-what-are-the-signs-and-why-leaders-get-exposed/?sh=4745dc0322ec2023.

2. Daniel Markovits, *The Meritocracy Trap: How America's Foundational Myth Feeds Inequality, Dismantles the Middle Class, and Devours the Elite* (New York: Penguin Random House, 2019).

3. Peggy McIntosh, "White Privilege: Unpacking the Invisible Knapsack," *Peace and Freedom*, July/August 1989, https://psychology.umbc.edu/wp-content/uploads/sites/57/2016/10/White-Privilege_McIntosh-1989.pdf.

## CONCLUSION

1. Gunnar Myrdal, *An American Dilemma* (London: Routledge, 2017).

2. James Clear, *Atomic Habits: An Easy & Proven Way to Build Good Habits & Break Old Ones* (New York: Avery, 2018).

3. Barry Deutsch, "The Male Privilege Checklist. An Unabashed Imitation of an Article by Peggy McIntosh," n.d., accessed August 7, 2023, https://xyonline.net/sites/xyonline.net/files/The Male Privilege Checklist.pdf.

4. RBC, "That Little Voice," YouTube, n.d., accessed November 7, 2023, https://youtu.be/Ll56imVATLk.

# Resources

Please follow this QR code to a comprehensive list of ID&E resources.

# Acknowledgments

## FROM EDDIE

I acknowledge the importance of family. To my brothers, Willie and Thomas; the legion of Pates scattered across this country; and to my family in and around Niederfischbach, Germany. A special shout-out to all the lovely dogs we've been fortunate to have in our lives. I've learned a ton about unconditional love from each of them.

I sincerely acknowledge Charles Stevens, who hired me right out of grad school in 2000, and trusted me to drive ID&E for his Microsoft organization, the Enterprise Partner Group.

Without that nod, who knows what path I would have ended up on. Charles, you also modeled an inclusive and empathetic leadership style that was the blueprint for my impact in this space. I am forever grateful.

Sean Kelley, bro! You've been there almost every single step of the way, and for that I can never thank you enough. You've pushed me to be real above all else and have modeled a servant leadership style that stands alone; and, in literally a thousand phone conversations, you've given me guidance, support, advice, and love that I can never repay.

There have also been too many other people to name who have supported me, partnered with me, and simply been there for me, but you know who you are, so please accept my heartfelt thanks. I also need to acknowledge every single team I was on and the amazing people I've led over the last twenty-three years, including my coauthor, Jonathan, because it was their passion and dedication that illuminated my journey. Wow—I can't help but smile when I think of each and every one of you.

I would be remiss if I didn't acknowledge Neal Maillet and Berrett-Koehler (BK). Neal, your engaging style and authentic interest in us, not just as writers, but as people, was very important to me. One of the best things that has come from writing our book is the realization of how special a publisher like BK is. The amount of energy and expertise we've experienced from the staff at BK Publishers has been incredible. Shout-out to Jeevan Sivasubramaniam, Katelyn Keating, Ashley Ingram, Daniel Tesser, Sarah Nelson, and Katie Sheehan. Your brilliance and passion are remarkable and have made my experience as a first-time author extraordinary.

Danielle Goodman, I can't thank you enough. Sometimes you get lucky in life, and we certainly were lucky having you as a writing coach. We definitely benefited greatly from your remarkable structural and writing suggestions, but it was your insightful challenges based on your lived experiences that made our book, and me as a writer, so much better. When all is said and done, we will owe you an amazing amount of credit.

Finally, I acknowledge all the ID&E professionals worldwide, who are fighting the fight every single day to make a difference. Thank you to all of you who have had a dilemma and are doing something about the fact that the credo of "inalienable rights for all" is clearly not true for the underestimated populations that face oppression day in and day out.

So many people have illuminated the path I've walked. We never do it alone.

## FROM JONATHAN

First and foremost, thank you to my family. To my partner in life, Stacie: none of my accomplishments in life would have happened without you. You are everything to me.

To my daughters, Katie and Jaclyn: a father couldn't be prouder than I am. You two inspire me every day. It is seeing what you've each accomplished that motivates me to continue to create and build.

To my mom, Marilyn Rogers Wax z"l:* you would be so proud and so thrilled to share this book with all your family and friends. Throughout your life, Mom, you exuded the heart, courage, and wisdom of a leader while always placing the highest value on family. We miss you dearly.

To Louise and Bill Halfon z"l: you believed in me before I believed in myself, and that inspired me to try to make a difference in this world. I wish you were here so I could hand you this book.

Thank you to my siblings, Jeffrey, Brian, and Ellen. I wouldn't be where I am today without your love, support, and guidance.

To Bill Price: simply said, this book would not have happened without you. You coached us on writing a book together and introduced us to Neal Maillet at Berrett-Koehler. Your partner, Lori, has been consistently and enthusiastically encouraging me to write this book since she heard the initial idea that sprung from my master's thesis.

---

* It is a Jewish tradition when mentioning someone who is no longer living to place the Hebrew acronym *z"l* after their name. It stands for *zikhrono/zikhronah livrakha*, meaning "May his/her memory be a blessing."

To my coauthor, Eddie: you hired me for your team after I had spent many years away from core ID&E work in a corporate environment, and I'm so grateful you did! After nearly five extraordinary years, we both left Amazon and together moved this book from a vision to reality.

Randy Massengale was the founder of the first diversity team at Microsoft in 1993 and became the company's first director of diversity. Randy took a chance on an energetic white guy with a passion for social justice and civil rights. He took me under his wing and made a commitment to teach me everything he knew about our discipline. Randy gave me the tools and resources to become credible in a field where white men are a minority. He changed my life immensely, helping me find my life's work and spend my career doing the work I love to do. Thank you, Randy.

A mountain of gratitude to Danielle Goodman of The GoodGood Editing, our writing development coach. Danielle is this book's elixir. She gracefully brought her well-honed knowledge, skills, and abilities to the text and, from a project management perspective, helped us successfully navigate our journey so that we arrived at our destination safely and on time.

Thank you to Neal Maillet at BK. Eddie and I are grateful for your enthusiastic support and belief in our vision. Your advice and guidance throughout were stellar. The endless stream of talent at BK is extraordinary. We are grateful to Jeevan Sivasubramaniam; Katelyn Keating; Ashley Ingram; Susan Geraghty; Lewelin Polanco; Daniel Tesser; Sarah Nelson; Katie Sheehan; freelance copyeditor, Michele Jones; and our photographer, Rishi Lakshminarayanan.

Thank you to all the people on teams I've led, the teams I've been fortunate to contribute to, and to the many leaders who guided my career. You were the source of much of the learning shared in this book.

# Index

trust
  with business partners, 20–21, 95
  destroying, 77–78
  establishing, 13, 97–98, 119–20, 128
  importance of, 27–28, 96
Turkey (country), 43
*The 21 Irrefutable Laws of Leadership*
    (Maxwell), 80–81

unconscious bias
  culture fit mentality and, 172–73
  defined, 46
  examples of, 46–47, 183–84
  mitigating, 49–51, 125–26, 138–40
  types of, 48–49
underestimated groups, 161, 193
underrepresented groups
  data and, 89, 97–98, 123
  employee referral groups and, 92
  mentoring and sponsorship, 98–101
  "replacement theory," 169
  talent acquisition of, 61, 93–95, 114
United States Supreme Court, 14

Valashiay, Rovina, 105
values, 27, 102, 116, 180–82
video tele-conference (VTC), 148–50
visibility, 101, 122–23, 132–33, 151
The Voice, 49–50

"volunteerism" of employees, 103,
    166–67
VTC (video tele-conference), 148–50
vulnerability, 31–32, 75–77, 100–101,
    128, 144
vulnerable employees, 22–23, 121–22,
    136–37

white privilege, 177–78, 178, 193–94,
    193–94
"White Privilege: Unpacking the
    Invisible Knapsack"
    (McIntosh), 193
"white savior," 100
white supremacy, 13–14
whole person, 78–80
wild ethnocentrism, 44–46
Wilke, Jeff, 105
wisdom, 33–34, 39–40, 52, 62
women
  bias against, 48–49, 55–56
  intersectionality and, 37–38
  in the workplace, 61, 64, 89–90, 92,
    115, 151
  See also Black women

Yeaman, Adetoun, 39

Zune (Microsoft), 43

# About the Authors

**Eddie Pate, PhD** (he/him/his) (right), writes about inclusion, diversity, and equity (ID&E). He has a doctorate in sociology from the University of Washington and a bachelor's degree in wildlife management from Humboldt State University, where he is a member of its athletic Hall of Fame for football. Eddie has spent seventeen years doing ID&E work for Microsoft, Starbucks, Avanade, and Amazon, primarily in leadership roles. He has also spent six years doing ID&E speaking and consulting via his consulting practice, Eddie Pate Speaking and Consulting; he is a sought-after speaker, facilitator, and guide who delivers in a way that speaks directly to everyone in the room. Eddie is a board member for the Institute for Sustainable Diversity and Inclusion and a member of the Microsoft Alumni Network board of trustees. He's married to Valeri with two kids, Karley and Arthur, and loves family above all. He is a dog person and loves traveling, photography, animals, and the natural world. He loves both time in the weight room and time spent staring reflectively at any body of water. He is inspired by good humans, empathy, diversity, global cultural differences, and the passion people show for peace, awareness, and love.

To contact Eddie directly, email eddiepate21@gmail.com or scan the following QR code with your phone.

**Jonathan Stutz, MA** (he/him/his) (left), is the founder and president for Global Diversity Partners Inc. He has over twenty-five years' experience working in leading-edge companies such as Amazon, Microsoft, and Zulily. Jonathan led ID&E for four international businesses within Amazon's Worldwide Operations group; and at Microsoft, he initially led ID&E for the Worldwide Sales and Support group, and later for the Worldwide Operations group.

As a community leader, Jonathan is a human services commissioner for the City of Kirkland, Washington, and serves on the board of trustees for Youth Eastside Services, a nonprofit based in Bellevue, Washington. Previously, he cofounded the Seattle area's Eastside Diversity Task Force and, separately, the Eastside Latino Leadership Forum. While at Microsoft, he cofounded the Professional Technical Diversity Network in Puget Sound and the Bay Area. Jonathan has served on the National Diversity Committee for the Society of Human

Resources Management (SHRM) and is a past president of SHRM's local Lake Washington chapter.

Jonathan earned his master's degree from City University of Seattle and his bachelor's in political science from the University of Washington. He is passionate about running, hiking, and spending as much time as possible with friends, family, and his cherished English Crème Golden Retriever, Simon. Born in Toronto, Canada, Jonathan spent formative years in Atlanta, Georgia, and Mercer Island, Washington. Today, Jonathan and his wife, Stacie, split time between Kirkland and Palm Desert, California. They are extremely proud of their two adult children, Dr. Katie Stutz and Jaclyn Stutz-Burrick, and their respective partners, Tom Sponheim and Aaron Stutz-Burrick.

To contact Jonathan directly, email jmstutz@gmail.com or scan the following QR code with your phone.

*Our book's website is inclusivepebbles.com.*

Dear reader,

Thank you for picking up this book and welcome to the worldwide BK community! You're joining a special group of people who have come together to create positive change in their lives, organizations, and communities.

## What's BK all about?

Our mission is to connect people and ideas to create a world that works for all.

Why? Our communities, organizations, and lives get bogged down by old paradigms of self-interest, exclusion, hierarchy, and privilege. But we believe that can change. That's why we seek the leading experts on these challenges—and share their actionable ideas with you.

## A welcome gift

To help you get started, we'd like to offer you a **free copy** of one of our bestselling ebooks:

### www.bkconnection.com/welcome

When you claim your **free ebook**, you'll also be subscribed to our blog.

## Our freshest insights

Access the best new tools and ideas for leaders at all levels on our blog at ideas.bkconnection.com.

Sincerely,

Your friends at Berrett-Koehler